A SEASON OF BIRDS

A Norfolk diary · 1911

ENDPAPERS A 1910 ordnance
survey map of the Hickling
area (scale: 1½ inches to
1 mile).

FRONTISPIECE A female
Montagu's harrier.

VINCENT AND LODGE

A SEASON
OF BIRDS

A Norfolk diary · 1911

Weidenfeld and Nicolson · London

Publisher's note

The four volumes of illustrated diary on which this book is based were produced privately, without any intention to publish. In condensing them into this single volume, a degree of selection has been necessary, not only for reasons of length but also to produce a consistently high quality of illustration and text. In order that this selection should not forfeit the importance of the diary as an ornithological record, a daily summary has been compiled of every bird sighting noted in the original diary, including information given on numbers, age and gender; this appears on pages 141–150, and is followed by an index of the birds illustrated or mentioned in this edition.

George Lodge's watercolours are reproduced here the same size as his originals, but the birds themselves are not to scale; in the original volumes, his illustrations are separated by the relevant diary entries. The informative notes on the birds, compiled by Edwin Vincent, have been added to give a brief introduction to the species, and relate specifically to the part they play in the bird life of the Hickling area; they are not intended as a general guide. Unless otherwise stated, the illustrations show adult males of those species with sexually differentiated plumage.

Edwin Vincent's introduction provides background information on many of the people and places mentioned in the diary; additional explanations have been inserted in square brackets in the diary itself.

The illustrations in the introduction are reproduced or supplied by kind permission of the following:
Christopher Cadbury 6 (right), 14
John Southern 6 (left)
Victoria & Albert Museum, photo by P. H. Emerson 9
Edwin Vincent 12, 15, 19 (left and right), 21 (left and right), 22, 23
The publishers are particularly grateful to Major Brian Booth, Christopher Cadbury and Edwin Vincent for their help in producing *A Season of Birds*.

First published in Great Britain by George Weidenfeld & Nicolson Limited 91 Clapham High Street London SW4

ISBN 0 297 77830 7

Colour separations by Newsele Litho Limited
Printed and bound in Italy by L.E.G.O., Vicenza

Contents

INTRODUCTION

My father, Jim Vincent, author of the diary which inspired this book, was born in the Norfolk village of Hickling in 1884. He was the fifth child, and first son, of Robert Vincent, a professional wildfowler and expert eel catcher, and his wife Rebecca. In those early days shooting and fishing were free on nearby Hickling Broad, Heigham Sounds and Horsey Mere, and the spoils went to the experts. When one man has to feed six or seven hungry mouths, then every shot has to tell, and only those who knew the tricks of the trade were able to keep going. There was also cash to be made from the shooting of rare birds and the taking of egg clutches for local collectors. My grandfather shot many rare birds; it was a way of life, and a means of finding money to bring up his family, but times since then have changed drastically, and preservation rather than persecution is now the order of the day.

It was only natural that my father, Jim, should follow in his father's footsteps and become an expert on the birds of Hickling. He and his brother William, born in 1885, would test each other's knowledge on winter evenings as, seated either end of a table, they asked each other to identify the species shown in an illustrated bird book. (William was unfortunately drowned on Hickling Broad on 30 January 1897, when he fell through the ice whilst retrieving a coot that my grandfather had shot.) It was my father's expertise, even as a youth of sixteen, that recommended him in 1900 to a visiting Cambridge undergraduate, the Hon. Edwin Montagu. A keen bird and egg collector, Mr Montagu engaged my father to assist him, with valuable results

Opposite, left George Edward Lodge (1860–1954), photographed *c.*1930 with a peregrine. Acknowledged by his fellow bird-painter Archibald Thorburn as an unequalled portrayer of birds of prey, his illustrations for Jim Vincent's diary reveal an unexpected flair for delicate watercolour studies of a great variety of species.

Opposite, right Jim Vincent (1884–1944), the author of the diary and head keeper of the White Slea Estate at Hickling, Norfolk, photographed in 1934 with some young bitterns.

7

that were well rewarded. It was the beginning of a relationship that was to transform my father's life and, in time, that of the Hickling area itself.

Hickling is one of the largest villages in the old East Flegg District and at the turn of the century consisted of approximately three hundred souls. The houses were scattered all over the village and the largest collection was in the area surrounding St Mary's Church, a fourteenth-century flint and stone building, in a three-sided block known as Town Street. Houses for the élite were situated on Hill Common, overlooking Hickling Broad, which at three miles long and one mile wide is the largest of the Norfolk Broads. The local squire, Mr George W. Neal, lived at Hickling Hall, and the principal landowner was Major John Digby Mills. About one-third of the parish was marsh and common land drained by water mills.

Community life centred on the three public houses, which were open from 6 a.m. until midnight, and St Mary's Church Hall, where local dances or political meetings were held. The majority of the working population earned their living as farm labourers, rush and reed cutters, or as fishermen, joining the herring boats at Great Yarmouth in September and returning only at Christmas when the local season ended. In those days, train-loads of girls from Scotland used to come and stay at Great Yarmouth for the herring season, and their job was to gut, salt and pack the vast quantities of fish in oak casks. After Christmas, a few locals would again join the herring fleet for other fields in Scotland, Hull, Grimsby and Milford Haven, as farm wages were very low: ten shillings for a sixty-hour week. Most people kept a pig, a goat and a few chickens in the back yard, and women would make their own bread from local white flour ground in a corn mill at Sutton, which they stored in large wooden bins.

Like the other young men of the village, my father took any job that was going, working for a time with a threshing tackle outfit, until, in his early twenties, he decided to train for the Methodist ministry. But he never

Opposite A photographic study of the Norfolk Broads entitled *A Rushy Shore*, c.1885 by P.H.Emerson.

completed his training, because in 1908 Mr Montagu came back to Hickling, with another friend and fellow bird-enthusiast, Lord Lucas, and once again sought the assistance of my father.

Edwin Montagu was by this time Liberal Member of Parliament for West Cambridgeshire. He had been born in London in 1879, the second son of the first Lord Swathling, a commanding figure in the Anglo-Jewish world who, as Samuel Montagu, represented Whitechapel in the House of Commons for fifteen years. Although never robust, Edwin Montagu's indomitable spirit and love of adventure led him to many parts of the world in his youth, to collect rare birds and their eggs. He read Natural Sciences at Cambridge, after which he trained briefly for the law before following his father into Parliament in 1906. Soon afterwards, he was made Secretary to Herbert Asquith, who was then Chancellor of the Exchequer; in 1910 he became Under-Secretary of State for India, and was the Secretary from 1917 to 1922.

When Mr Montagu saw Hickling again in 1908, his attitude to the bird life changed, and both he and Lord Lucas (who was also a member of Asquith's government) decided to become conservers of rare birds rather than collectors. They enjoyed shooting, but confined it to duck, coot, snipe and other more common species. (Ornithologists often decry the shooting man, yet some of the best ornithologists I have met have also shot; they at least knew what they were aiming at, and respected the rare birds that hove in sight.) In 1909 they were joined by Sir Edward Grey, then Foreign Secretary in the Liberal government, and a keen sportsman. Together they rented White Slea Lodge Estate from its owner, Major Mills, and financed its maintenance as a shoot.

It was as a keeper of this estate that my father was employed by Edwin Montagu, to establish the habitats that would encourage and preserve migrating birds in the spring and summer, and develop ducks and other fowl for the shooting season in the winter. He lived in a rent-free estate cottage near Hickling Church, and his wage was £1.10s.0d per week. In 1909 my father married Ruth Naomi Bell, a local teacher, and I was their first child, born in July 1910; my brother Ivor was born in May 1920. The cottage was small, with three bedrooms, two downstairs rooms and a pantry; there was no electric light or sanitation until 1930, and oil lamps, candles and coal cooking stoves were the order of the day.

In winter my father would be out working from about 8 a.m. to 4 p.m., but in spring and summer months it was a daylight to dusk operation. He would cycle one mile from our home to the Pleasure Boat Inn, on the edge of the Broad, collect his punt and wander off across the Broad to White Slea Lodge, a distance of three miles (the only approach by land was by a rough cart track; until this was replaced by a cinder ash road in 1928, all visitors to the Lodge were met at the Inn and ferried over the water). In the spring, my father would be out at dawn looking for rare birds and their nests, only returning late at night. In May 1913, there was a purported visit in the Horsey area of a snowy owl, and he stayed out the whole of one moonlit night hoping to see the bird. This led to suspicious accusations from my mother that never died!

My father always said that although Edwin Montagu was of another denomination, he was the kindest of masters any man could have. He always appealed to the best in those he employed, and recognized it when they gave it. His practical sympathy to his employees can best be illustrated by an example I often heard repeated by my father. On a visit to Hickling, Mr Montagu's chauffeur was taken ill; just before he died, my father sent a telegram to Mr Montagu, and received the following reply: 'Give my love to White and thank him for all his services to me. Tell him I will promise to look after his wife and five children.' My father said that the dying man was overjoyed with this message. The promise was faithfully kept, even by means of a trust fund after Edwin Montagu's own early death in 1924.

Edwin Montagu and his two partners used to visit Hickling with their friends as often as their duties permitted, especially in the winter for the shooting and in the spring to see the rare birds; and in 1912 Lord Lucas bought a house in the area, Horsey Hall. All three gentlemen were with my father when one of the first exciting finds was made on 28 April 1910: the nest of a Montagu's harrier (named after a nineteenth-century naturalist, Col. George Montagu), containing a single, bluish-white egg about the size of a pigeon's egg. This bird of prey, about the size of a rook, comes from South Africa and southern Spain; it had not been seen at Hickling since 1883, and had never nested in Norfolk. After the find, a hut was quickly placed nearby and two full-time watchers from the estate were employed to guard the nest. After ten weeks, three youngsters took flight. The following year, four Montagu's harrier nests were found, and it was assumed that the two old birds plus the youngsters, each with a mate, had returned. Since that date, the harrier has been a regular visitor and has spread to other areas of Norfolk and Suffolk.

Another important discovery in these early years was that of a young bittern, found on 7 July 1911 at nearby Sutton by my father and Miss Emma L. Turner, an amateur bird photographer. The last bittern to have been seen in the area had been shot in August 1886, twenty-five years before. Since 1911 it has increased and spread to other parts of Norfolk and neighbouring counties. Jim always regarded this as his most thrilling find, and later wrote and broadcast about 'The Romance of the Bittern'.

It was undoubtedly these early and memorable sightings that inspired Edwin Montagu to put together the four volumes of the 1911 diary on which this present book is based. I have diaries kept by my father from 1912 to 1944, but did not know of this earlier record until recently. Whether or not Mr Montagu also asked my father to keep a diary in the first place, I do not know; but he was certainly responsible for the most striking feature of the

Opposite, left to right
Robert Vincent, Sir Edward Grey, Jim Vincent, Linkhorn (a keeper) and Edwin Montagu pose with their bag and retrievers outside White Slea Lodge after a successful day's duck shooting.

Miss Emma Turner (photographed *c*.1890), an amateur bird photographer who lived on a houseboat at Hickling for twenty-five years. She developed her sepia photographs in a small shed built on an island still known as Miss Turner's island, opposite Swim Coots. Edwin Vincent recalls: 'Miss Turner was small in stature but very wiry, quite capable with a punt or rowing boat, and always of a cheerful disposition.'

Opposite The first Montagu's harriers to be born in Norfolk, photographed in 1910 by Miss Emma Turner.

1911 volumes, the illustrations. These are the work of George Edward Lodge, one of the best-known bird painters of the period and a frequent guest of Edwin Montagu at Hickling.

George Lodge was first and foremost a great naturalist, who also had the gift of accurately portraying the birds he knew so well. In order to make the watercolours and pencil drawings for my father's diary, he would have used his usual method, field observation followed by work in his studio, which he described in his autobiography, *Memoirs of an Artist Naturalist*, written in 1946 at the age of eighty-five: 'The movements of birds . . . are so lively that it takes a very quick eye to see and know what one is looking at, and what a bird is really doing. The only way is to make sketches as rapidly as possible and afterwards make the best one can of a bad sketch. Errors can often be rectified at leisure without spoiling the freshness of a sketch from life.' Although a master of taxidermy (he stuffed his first bird, an owl, at the age of twelve), he did not use mounted specimens for his artistic work because they lacked the grace of the living bird. However, he did use his knowledge as a taxidermist to achieve scientifically correct details of plumage. He illustrated a number of scientific books, most notably *The Birds of the British Isles*, a twelve-volume work by David Bannerman, and usually used tempera, not watercolour. He continued painting until shortly before his death in February 1954, at the age of ninety-three; in his obituary, David Bannerman described Lodge as 'a wonderful example of the best that Britain can produce, a sportsman, a naturalist and a very fine gentleman'.

To illustrate my father's diary, George Lodge chose one incident from each day's entry and then portrayed the bird, or birds, in the habitat and circumstances in which they had been observed. In over 150 watercolours and a similar number of pencil drawings, he shows nearly 150 different species, including rare birds such as the bittern, marsh harrier and Montagu's harrier – an indication of the richness of the bird life at that time.

Mr Montagu and his two friends were determined to make Hickling into a paradise for birds, and how well they succeeded is a tribute to their devotion. A list of the rarest birds recorded at Hickling between 1910 and 1944 is included in this book in an appendix, but, to mention just two more important developments, in 1915 the marsh harrier returned to breed at Hickling after many years' absence (the few my father records in his 1911 diary were visitors only); and the bearded tit or 'reed pheasant', also at a low ebb, was encouraged and has since spread through the eastern counties. The protection of birds such as the Montagu's or marsh harrier could raise serious problems; for example, local gamekeepers, whose carefully reared birds were the harriers' natural prey, had to be prevented from trying to retaliate. A record kept in 1912 of one nesting pair of Montagu's harriers shows they made a total of some 2,000 visits to bring food for their young; and it can be assumed that a further 2,000 head of game would have been required to feed adults and offspring between the time they left the nest and their departure for Africa in September. This is a staggering total for one pair, let alone the seven pairs of Montagu's harriers and three of marsh harriers I have seen raise their young in one season in the Hickling and Horsey area.

In his lifetime, my father recorded 247 different species of birds at Hickling. Providing the necessary habitat for such a variety of birds is an art that requires many years of study. It must be remembered that birds are not just passing migrants who suddenly decide to drop in for a season; they are reconnaissance experts who stay and continue to visit annually only when the habitat is to their liking. Harriers, for example, require rough reed beds; bitterns, bearded tits and reed warblers, thin reed beds; waders, shovelers and garganey, flooded pools on low marshes; ruffs, wagtails, plovers and short-eared owls, dry grassy marshland. The construction and maintenance of these different terrains required money as well as encouragement, and my father was very fortunate in his employers, who gave him every opportunity to improve the flora and fauna of the estate. The Hon. Ivor Grenfell, who became a member of the White Slea shooting syndicate in 1920, took over the hire of the land in 1924 after the premature death of Edwin Montagu. Unfortunately he was killed two years later when motoring home on a foggy evening. His father, Lord Desborough (William Henry Grenfell), became my father's next employer; after visiting the area his son had talked about so much, he decided to take over the estate. Lord Desborough was one of the most famous all-round athletes England has ever produced. When loading for his Lordship, I have seen him, at the age of seventy-seven, kill a right and left at partridges, firing from his right shoulder, and seen him repeat this performance firing from his left shoulder: a most unusual and unforgettable performance.

The habitats my father worked hard to construct were from the beginning under threat of both natural and man-made disruption. Hickling Broad, Heigham Sounds and Horsey Mere have always been affected by conditions in the North Sea; even without any rain, if the wind changes to a north-westerly direction at the new or full moon, there can be a two-foot rise or more in water levels. If this change of wind is accompanied by heavy rain, there is flooding. White Slea Lodge was for many years subject to internal flooding during the spring and winter high tides, and six inches of water indoors was quite common. It rested on boggy marshland and, although the base had been fortified in earlier years with faggots, these would have rotted away with the passage of time, allowing the foundations to settle. On one occasion, when staying at the Lodge in October 1927, Lord Desborough got out of bed in the morning and stepped into six inches of water. This prompted him to begin a rebuilding programme, the following year, in which the original pine-wood lounge was jacked up and the remainder rebuilt on a similar style to the old property.

In recent years, a more serious threat has been the proposal to construct a barrier dam, either in Great Yarmouth harbour or further downstream. This would quickly change conditions in all the high-level systems, which include the Broads, the dykes connecting them, and the marshy lands bordering on them, locally known as randes. On the randes grow sedge reeds, used for ridging on thatched roofs; wild parsley, the home of the rare swallow-tailed butterfly; and the bulrush, used years ago by the coopering trade, and now the favourite habitat of the bearded tit. If a barrier dam were installed at Great Yarmouth, the surge of flood water would be halted, enabling marshes which now get flooded at high tide to be ploughed up for agricultural use. This would cause the loss of the present flora and fauna, including many species of little wading birds. The whole character of the area would change, a matter of concern not only to the naturalist but also to summer visitors. There is already less water than in the days of my youth, since when many areas have become overgrown with reeds and weeds. It has been suggested that these waterways should be opened up, and that the Broads should become a National Park. Viewing Hickling now in the eventide of life, I should like to think it were possible to halt the deterioration and restore it to how it was when I lived and worked there in my youth. But the conservationists have acted many years too late, and the expense would now be prohibitive.

In my youth at Hickling, it was my good fortune to meet some of the finest ornithologists, bird artists and bird photographers this country has known. They came to meet my father, who had become a legend in his lifetime. I well remember Lord William Percy, who was photographing the bittern on his private estate, Catfield Hall. He brought the first photographs to show my father, all of which showed only the female bittern at the nest, and said that when he next came he would bring a photograph of male and female on the nest together. My father looked at him quietly, and said: 'My Lord, I am not a rich man but I will bet you £5 that you cannot bring me a picture of both

Opposite A bittern at the nest, photographed by Miss Turner in 1920.

18

birds at the nest.' His Lordship, certain of success, replied that he would bet £10 to my father's £5 that he would get the picture; they shook hands on it, and his Lordship left. About two weeks later, he returned to our house, placed two white £5 notes on the table, and asked my father how he was so certain that he would never get the picture. 'I will ask your Lordship one question,' my father replied. 'Did you ever see a cock pheasant on the nest?' His Lordship replied that, of course not, a cock pheasant is polygamous. My father picked up the two fivers, smiled and said, 'My Lord, I have proved that the male bittern is polygamous but it took me twenty years to find it out.' His Lordship gracefully acknowledged defeat.

Another incident that reveals something of my father's knowledge concerns two American ornithologists who visited my father one spring. Standing with them on the lawn at White Slea Lodge, my father remarked that for the past three days there had been an osprey in the Hickling area, and that he hoped they might see it again that day. He then gazed around, and said, 'There is the osprey sitting on that dead tree in Heigham Sounds Wood.' As this was at least three-quarters of a mile away, the two Americans had to use a telescope and a large pair of binoculars to pick out the spot my father was indicating. Sure enough, there was the osprey; and the two visitors were amazed at what they thought was my father's marvellous eyesight. What they did not know, but Jim did, is that ospreys sit only on dead (and therefore leafless) trees, which give them the best vantage point. As the osprey is such a large bird, its outline on the dead branch in the Sounds Wood was clearly visible to the naked eye, once you knew where to look.

One of my most treasured sightings occurred one Saturday evening, 9 May 1936, when, about to set off for a local dance, I was asked by my father to go down to White Slea to check that all was quiet on the Broads. I set off on my motor cycle, interested only in the fact that I would be late for the dance. When I arrived at the Lodge, I went up the Look-out with a pair of binoculars. Suddenly I saw a bittern fly past, within fifty yards of me. It alighted on a raised bed of dead rushes, and then what seemed the impossible happened: I saw, for the only time in my life, the bittern actually boom. I watched its actions, I was thrilled, I even forgot the dance. The bird repeated the manœuvre three times before eventually flying away. I dashed home to tell my father exactly what I had seen; after hearing my description, he said: 'Treasure that sighting, Edwin, you may never see it again. I saw it myself twenty years ago, and I don't ever expect to see it again. By your description of the actions of the bird, which are identical to those I saw, I know you have seen the bittern boom.' It was not merely the sound of the boom which had so excited my father and me; this mating call is fairly common on the Broads between early March and mid-April. It was rather the chance to *see* this most secretive bird's performance. To make the sound, it gives two or three preliminary short grunts, with the head at an angle of 45 degrees, filling the lungs with air; it then lowers its head to ground level, neck extended, and it is the exhalation of the air that creates the booming sound. The manœuvre is repeated three or four times. On a still evening this resonant sound can be heard at a distance of two miles.

One of the most plentiful birds on Hickling Broad in the winter months was the coot. They used to arrive at night from the Continent, flying only when there was a full moon, and it was possible to cross the Broad in the late afternoon and see no more than 500 coots on the water, but revisit it in the morning and find some 2–3,000. For many years it was the custom to hold an annual Coot Shoot in late January or early February when birds were most plentiful. Some famous people have taken part in these shoots, including King George vi, George Lodge and Sir Peter Scott. Several sportsmen have seen their renown as game shoots utterly destroyed as, bobbing around in a boat on the choppy water, they have tried to shoot a coot doing a side-slipping act in the high wind.

The record bag of **1,275** head was achieved by seventeen guns on 10 February 1934 with the following result:

1,213 coot	1 scaup duck
14 pochard duck	1 shoveler duck
10 mallard duck	27 mute swans
7 tufted duck	2 moorhens

The residents of Hickling and the surrounding villages looked forward to these shoots, as all the birds were given away at the end of the day. Coots, which are skinned, not plucked, are very rich in protein, and they were issued on the basis of one bird per member of each household. It was possible to give away 1,000 head of game in an hour, but one always had to watch that a second member of the same household did not join the queue for another allocation.

In 1930, after the shooting season was over, my father decided to attempt to learn more about the migratory pattern of the wild mallard by catching them on the flight ponds and ringing them (he was one of the pioneers of the now widespread practice of ringing birds). The results of his experiment showed that there was movement from the south-east and the east towards the north and north-east in the late autumn, and back again in the spring months, across the narrow part of the North Sea; and they also exploded the fallacy that the migratory habits of birds are governed by the direction of the wind (the main factor is the climatic conditions at the point of departure). I consider that, although wind has some effect, it is not as important as many ornithologists still believe; although a bird cannot fly in the teeth of a gale, it can travel very close to any reasonable wind.

The White Slea Estate was always, until 1944, semi-public, but fortunately most egg collectors were sporting enough to leave it alone. In my father's experience, well-intentioned bird-lovers disturbed many more rare nests,

week after the Big Coot Drive

I have given away for my employer over 24000 coot during the last 20 years.

The annual Shoot is mainly held in Feb and as the time draws near feelers are sent out such as "I hear there is going to be a Coot Shoot on such a date" There is a move to draw me to say yes or no.

In the old days there was not much organisation but anyone who could mount a battery of various bores of muzzle loaders, and find some one up to "shove" him (a Norfolk term for punt) went to the shoot.

At one shoot the police raided the fleet as they came ashore for licences. One man passed in to the Inn, slid his loaded gun in the corner of a room, and came out looking very innocent and chuckling

to himself on how he had outwitted the police. But a small boy of the house saw the gun standing in the corner and played upon the trigger when bang goes the gun discharging both barrels through the ceiling and the charge of shot lodged in the mattress of the bed upstairs. This completely gave away the owner of the gun to the police and it cost him a bit extra for damages.

Today invitations are sent out to 16 guns with a reserve list to draw from if any fail. The same number of good punters are secured for the guns with 4 others in the rear as pickers up. This is no easy matter to adjust as certain guns want certain punters and some of the punters favour

The medal awarded to Jim Vincent, 'bird watcher and bird protector', by the Royal Society for the Protection of Birds.

through photographic attempts, too much sight-seeing or misplaced steps, than egg collectors. This is even truer today: many naturalists must now see the nest as well as the bird to believe that it exists; and once a rare one is publicized, scores of enthusiasts descend on the area, regardless of the consequences. The estate has continued to be protected, however. After Lord Desborough's death in 1944, it was taken over by his two daughters, Lady Salmond and Lady Imogen Gage, and in 1946 they sold their interest to the Norfolk Naturalists Trust, who own it today. There are sponsored water nature trails and walks, and White Slea now gets its financial support from the sale of reeds for thatching and the donations of various benefactors and members of the Trust. Sadly, this is not enough for the upkeep of the estate along the lines of my father's day, and the main loss has been in the number of wild duck, chiefly mallard, pochard and tufted duck. Shooting is forbidden, and so there is less interest in encouraging these winter visitors; and some years ago hundreds of mute swans were allowed to reside and breed at Hickling, with the result that they ate all the natural duck weeds and polluted the water – a problem made worse by the thousands of gulls which now use Hickling Broad as a resting place each night.

Although my father was justly renowned as a great ornithologist (he was presented with an illuminated scroll and a Gold Medal by the Royal Society for the Protection of Birds in appreciation of his work), he was also an excellent game and clay pigeon shot. In 1933 he won the Daily Telegraph Sporting Championship Cup with a score of 93 kills out of possible 100. In the following year he was the first to record the maximum score at skeet shooting, i.e. twenty birds, twenty different angles, twenty shots, and for this achievement he was presented with a Gold Badge by the Clay Pigeon Shooting Association.

The highlight of my father's career as an ornithologist and naturalist occurred in 1930, when he was invited to stay at Sandringham for three days as the guest of King George V. He was greatly honoured to have several long talks with His Majesty, who asked many questions about birds and about Hickling in particular. After my father returned home, he sent King George a watercolour by J. C. Harrison of avocets, and he received a most charming letter from the King's Private Secretary, Sir Derek Keppel, accepting the picture and enclosing a signed photograph of His Majesty which he had been commanded to send as a souvenir of the visit to Sandringham. This always held pride of place in my father's home and is still treasured by my family.

My father died in the early hours of 4 November 1944, aged only sixty, in a Norwich nursing home. I was alone with him at the time, and silently watched as his life ebbed peacefully away. At the precise moment of his passing, the stillness was broken by the chattering of sparrows in the trough outside the window. This continued for a full minute before all went quiet again. I have always believed that this was birdland saying a last farewell to their devoted friend. Jim loved the birds, and I know that this was the tribute he would have valued above all others.

His 1911 diary gives but a glimpse of the personality of my father. Those who knew him well recall his modesty, his generosity, the warmth of his welcome and his kindness to all who sought his advice on birds. It has been my pleasure to write this introduction because it has enabled me not only to pay my personal tribute to him, but also to acknowledge the great debt of gratitude we owe to his three mentors, the Hon. Edwin Montagu, Lord Lucas and Sir Edward Grey, who started the Hickling Broad Sanctuary. This book is also of great value as an ornithological record of the return of the bittern and Montagu's harrier as nesting species. I hope every reader will enjoy 'A Season of Birds', written in 1911 by Jim Vincent of Hickling.

Edwin Vincent

JANUARY

—⟶ 1st ⟵—

Saw the old male Goldeneye on Hickling [*Broad*].

—⟶ 2nd ⟵—

Strong wind from N.W. Squalls of hail. No-one in
Hickling can remember so high a tide.

I saw close by the [*White Slea*] Lodge on Hickling
wall a Richard's Pipit. Watched it running on
the wall, and at the edge of water several
minutes. Was attracted by its loud note first. It
looked almost the size of a Redwing as it flew
along.

—⟶ 3rd ⟵—

Mr Russell [*a local landowner*], Mr Warre and
myself saw female Hen-harrier, adult male
Goldeneye with some immatures, Bearded Tits,
a good number of Pochard, some Tufties [*Tufted
Duck*], Shovelers, and a few Mallard.

GOLDENEYE *(2 adult males with immatures)* *A winter
visitor to Hickling; sometimes called a 'whistler' because
of the sound of its wings in flight. A fairly uncommon
and solitary duck, seldom seen in parties of more than
five or six.*

—⟶ 4th ⟵—

We saw Bearded Tits close by Lodge, but there
are few about compared with us in the nesting
season. This being due I think to their distribu-
tion over other Broads during winter, where few,
if any, in some places nest.

—⟶ 5th ⟵—

Very light breeze from E. Milder.
Went on Heigham Sounds after breakfast,
obtained

2 Pochard
1 Tufted Duck
Gibbs Wood 1 Rabbit

Saw a Black-throated Diver (immature) come
flying from Hickling on to Heigham Sounds.

—⟶ 7th ⟵—

Gave Messrs Ashys a day on Hickling:

Bag 2 Pochard
35 Coots
—————
37 Head

Saw a flock of **300** Pochard in Ball's Corner, the **20**
immature Goldeneyes, and the adult Goldeneye.

⟣ 9th ⟣

Saw a Snow Bunting on the marshes. It looked a very good bird.

⟣ 10th ⟣

Saw a Great Grey Shrike at the end of White Slea wall. It kept flying to, and perching on some small bushes on the marsh. After a time it flew across to some hedgerows, and hovered over them, as a Kingfisher would over water. Never saw it take anything.

Saw a Merlin chasing a Skylark, but never captured it.

Saw the adult Goldeneye in company with 30 immatures.

⟣ 11th ⟣

Saw the female Hen-harrier in the marshes, close by Lodge.

⟣ 13th ⟣

Wind N.W. Squalls of hail and snow.

Saw 10 Geese flying over Heigham Sounds. They settled on some marshes known as Martham Holmes. They were probably Bean Geese.

Saw the adult Goldeneye alone on Heigham Sounds.

A Waxwing in excellent plumage was shown to me. It was shot on some allotments at Potter Heigham by a fisherman. I asked him not to shoot any others if he saw them.

⟣ 14th ⟣

Saw 14 Sheldrakes on Hickling Broad. There were 6 females.

There looked to be an increase of Coots in Hickling too.

⟣ 16th ⟣

The edges of the Broad are frozen, thus all the Coots are in the open water, and there look to be quite a good number, though I have seen more, but there was nothing less than 2,000.

Saw a Grey Wagtail and a Waxwing to-day.

⟣ 17th ⟣

The Hickling Broad is frozen nearly over with the exception of about 2 acres against Pleasure Island, where the Coots, Pochard and other things are in.

They look a black mass from White Slea Look-out.

GREY WAGTAIL *(top)* *A rare visitor to Norfolk, more frequently found where running streams abound, particularly in Scotland, Wales and Ireland. Like all wagtails, it is characterized by a wagging tail, undulating flight and scurrying gait. Usually has two broods in a season.*

RICHARD'S PIPIT *(bottom)* *A rare visitor, with a lark-like appearance, which breeds in southern France and Spain. Best distinguished by its length of limb and extremely long hind claw, generally longer than the toe. Named after the Frenchman who first identified the bird.*

Shot 12 Pigeons coming in to roost in Town Wood. The crop of one contained

2,671 clover blades
13 kernels barley
8 kernels wheat
7 pieces of grit
—————
2,699

Saw 2 Hawfinches; these are rare with us. Also 3 Green Woodpeckers chasing each other in the Town Wood.

⟹ 18th ⟸

The ice is breaking up on Hickling. There are a good number of Coots, 2,000 quite.

Saw a Common Scoter, 2 adult Goldeneyes, 30 immatures, and 400 or 500 Pochard which flew off to Horsey, as we came across Broad.

⟹ 20th ⟸

Have seen 2 Smews on Hickling to-day, both alike in plumage. Nudd [*Alfred Nudd, another keeper*] and I punted within 25 yards of one and watched it fishing by the edge of reed.

HAWFINCH *A rare visitor to Hickling, shown here in summer dress; in winter, the bill is yellow. It feeds on haws (hence its name), beechmast, berries and cherry stones, which are crushed by the powerful bill.*

Have never seen an old male, and Nudd stated he has never seen one on the Broad. No doubt they are young birds of the year which occur here.

Saw a Rough-legged Buzzard mobbed by Rooks and Crows.

21st

Have seen a few Mallard about, and believe several of them have paired off.

Seen a good number of Pochard on Hickling. They do not like leaving the Broad in foggy weather. They have been driving about low and in all directions these last few days.

Billy George [*a worker on the estate*] said there were 100 on White Slea this morning.

Have never been out darker nights than what they have been since Thursday.

22nd

Calm cold hazy day.

Saw 3 Geese come flying over the village about 50 yards high. They looked like White-fronted, but was hardly near enough for certainty.

23rd

There are hundreds of Pochard on Hickling, some of this is due, because they have shot 2 days on Horsey Mere. They had a Coot Shoot too, but only killed 36, so the head keeper told me.

24th

Strong wind from W.

Saw a Snow Bunting on the small marsh of Mr Russell's.

Saw 6 Golden Plovers in one flock to-day, but these birds are scarce with us, as we have no suitable grounds for them. There have been immense quantities of these at Horsey, and around Yarmouth.

25th

Light breeze from S.W. Mild.

There are a good number of Bullfinches about.

Saw a Great Spotted Woodpecker in White Slea Wood.

The water is gone down considerably, and there are several Snipe about on the randes [*the borders of the Broads*] and marshes.

Saw a flock of 10 Bearded Tits against White Slea.

Saw the female Hen-harrier against Lodge.

26th

Wind W. Very mild and warm.

The Coots are betaking themselves to the reed bushes this weather, some of them are beginning to pair off.

There are close on 2,000 yet on the Broad, and 500 to 600 Pochard, Tufties, Goldeneyes, but very few Mallard.

27th

The Mistle Thrushes are pairing off, they are very quarrelsome in the Woods.

Saw a pair of Green Woodpeckers in the Town Wood, also a pair of Kestrels.

The farmers and myself had a turn at Wood-pigeons in the evening: 26 were killed and picked up; 17 of these I killed in Town Wood.

28th

Calm sunny day; foggy evening.

Lord Lucas, Mr and Miss Russell came.

There are a lot of Pochard and Coots on Hickling.

Saw 2 adult Goldeneyes with quite 30 immatures.

29th

His Lordship and others saw Green Woodpecker in Gibbs Wood.

I saw the Smew fly and settle close by the edge of Pleasure Island. Have noticed this bird seldom alights more than 30 yards from edge of reeds, have never seen it settle on the centre of Broad.

POCHARD *(left) Referred to locally as a 'poker' (the male) or 'dun bird' (the female), this duck breeds chiefly in northern and eastern Europe although some stay to breed in Norfolk. Not as plentiful in Hickling now as in 1911.*

GREEN WOODPECKER *(right) Known in Norfolk as a 'yaffle' because of its call, which sounds like distant laughter. Nests in a hole made in a decaying tree.*

⟾ 30th ⟾

Strong wind from E. Very cold.

Lord Lucas and I went on [*Heigham*] Sounds, but saw few Pochard.

After breakfast went round to Ball's Corner, where we saw plenty of Pochard, a Gadwall was with them.

Saw several Snipe which sat very well indeed.

$$
\begin{array}{r}
\text{Drove Coots, and picked up } 28 \\
\text{Tuesday picked up } 5 \\
\text{Bagged Snipe } 7 \\
\hline
40
\end{array}
$$

His Lordship killed all with the exception of 4 Coots.

Saw old Goldeneyes with the immatures.

⟾ 31st ⟾

Saw 12 Widgeon, 7 Shovelers, the Smew on Hickling.

Picked up 5 Coots of yesterday's shooting.

Have many flocks of Peewits [*Lapwings*] going S., also Redwings, Larks [*Skylarks*], and Fieldfares. This no doubt means frost following.

There are plenty of Snipe about to-day.

FIELDFARE *(left) Known in Norfolk as a 'fulfer', and a regular winter visitor. The harsh cry of a flock in flight makes it very noticeable.*

WHITE-FRONTED GOOSE *(right) A winter visitor to Norfolk, sometimes called the 'laughing goose'.*

FEBRUARY

1st

Sharp frost; very calm. Broad is frozen over with the exception of an open place against Little Pleasure Island.

There are a great quantity of Pochard and Coots in the wake, probably 3,000 in all. They appear as a black mass.

2nd

Light breeze from N.W. There was a sharp frost last night, not so sharp as previous night.

There were quite 100 Coots, and about the same number of Pochard. 3 Smew came flying past within 25 yards, should say they were immature.

Several flocks of Peewits are about to-day. This looks like frost breaking up.

GREAT SPOTTED WOODPECKER *A fairly scarce bird of retiring habits which frequents most wooded areas in Britain. It nests in a hole made in a branch or trunk of a tree; both sexes take part in the incubation. In the breeding season the male makes a loud vibrating noise by rapidly hammering with his strong bill on the bark of a hollow tree. Its food consists of tree insects and their larvae, and various berries found in woodlands in autumn.*

3rd

The ice is breaking up fast and will all be gone off the Broad some time to-night.

Saw a Great Grey Shrike fly across to White Slea Wood; I went across about an hour later and came unexpectedly across the bird, which had been feeding upon a female Stonechat.

4th

Saw the female Hen-harrier and 3 Merlins, unless it was the same bird three times over.

6th

Saw quite 40 immature Goldeneyes on Hickling, there was only one adult male amongst them.

Saw 3 Great Crested Grebes, probably these are returned for breeding.

7th

There are quite 1,000 Black-headed Gulls congregated on the Broad from the land late in the afternoon; they then go off to sea for the night.

8th

Saw 2 Great Spotted Woodpeckers at Hickling.

There seem to be rather more than the usual number of Water Rails about; one hears them screaming all about the marshes.

There is only one adult male Goldeneye with the immatures now.

————— 9th —————

Saw 19 Mallard in one lot fly off Hickling.

There were about 40 Pochard on White Slea this morning, and saw close to 100 Pochard and Tufties on Hickling. There are close on 2,000 Coots too.

Saw the female Hen-harrier close to the Town Wood.

————— 10th —————

Very sharp frost in the morning, part of the Broad frozen. Wind S.

SMEW (top) *Not a common visitor, and the smallest of the three saw-billed ducks which frequent Britain. It is an excellent diver, but walks with difficulty owing to the backward position of the legs. Its food consists of small fish, which it catches securely with its serrated bill, and crustacea.*

TUFTED DUCK (bottom) *The most common of the diving ducks. It dives freely and frequently, feeding on weeds, water-beetles and small crustacea, and when pairs are together the female invariably takes off first. It is often in the company of other diving ducks, yet when mixed bunches of divers rise from the water they separate into species for flight.*

Saw 4 Teal and 5 Widgeon on Hickling and quite 400 to 500 Pochard.

In Gibbs Wood flushed a Woodcock against the drive. Saw 2 Short-eared Owls sitting in the young fir trees.

Saw about 80 Pochard and Tufties on Sounds, and 2 Dabchicks.

————— 11th —————

Wind N.W. Rain in morning, snow in afternoon.

The Black-headed Gulls, of which there are over 1,000, and over 200 Herring Gulls sleep on Hickling all night. One can hear them at night. This morning I was across just as it was getting light, and came across them. They covered nearly an acre and made a deafening noise with their wings and cries.

Saw a Great Spotted Woodpecker at Potter Heigham.

————— 13th —————

Sharp frost this morning. Greater part of Broad frozen over.

There looked a great number of Coots on the Broad this morning, as the frost drives them all from the reed beds where a good number get to at this time of year.

There is quite a dearth of surface-feeding ducks, and has been the whole year.

Saw the adult male Goldeneye with 30 immatures on Hickling.

14th

Saw a pair of Kestrels around their old nesting tree in Town Wood.

Have noticed along the hedgerows an unusual number of Golden-crested Wrens [*Goldcrests*] to-day. Probably they are migrating back.

Saw 4 Smews come past the Lodge unto Hickling Broad.

15th

There are quite 400 to 500 Pochard on Hickling. But they take themselves off part of the day either to Horsey or to sea.

There are a great number of Coots getting to the reed beds, some of them I believe have paired off.

Saw a decoy duck's nest with 16 eggs in.

WOODCOCK *(top) Arrives as a winter migrant in late October; very occasionally some will stay and breed in plantations. In England the woodcock has a reputation for 'airlifting' the young between its legs before they can fly. A solitary bird, it hunts for its food at dusk and at night. When flushed, it travels with a zig-zag flight.*

PINTAIL *(bottom, male and female) Known locally from the length of its tail as the 'sea pheasant', this elegant and solitary bird mixes with other surface-feeding ducks but is never seen in a large flock. It has never been known to nest at Hickling.*

16th

Saw the Great Grey Shrike on the same marsh where I saw it on January 10th.

Peewits are flocking about to-day as if frost is coming.

Saw 2 Green and a Great Spotted Woodpecker in the Town Wood.

17th

The Hon. E. S. Montagu and Mr G. E. Lodge shot today, bagging

14	Coots
11	Mallard
7	Snipe (Jack)
1	Pigeon
33	Head

We saw a pair of Pintails, several Teal, about 12 Shovelers, 2 Widgeon, 5 Smews, besides Golden-eyes, Tufties and Pochard.

18th

Very strong wind from W.S.W.

Coot Shoot to-day, 16 guns of our party.

Bag 132	Coots
3	Mallard
2	Pochard
1	Peewit
138	

There were 24 other guns on the outskirts looking out for birds leaving the Broad, and can only ascertain of 35 Coots being accounted for by this number. Some half dozen were armed with muzzle loaders. One used a 410 bore, another 22 short rifle.

19th

Strong wind from west with squalls.
Owing to strong wind, birds are not moving about very much.
Saw Widgeon come by Lodge, a few Pochard, Goldeneyes and Tufties on Hickling.

28th

Snipe are drumming. Peewits tippling about, and a few Redshanks are whistling about, reminding one of warmer days to come.
I love to hear the Redshanks when they first arrive, but they get on my nerves at times before they go.

LAPWING *(left) Named after the flapping sound of its wings in flight; also known as a peewit, after its cry, or green plover. In spring, the males perform striking displays, rising and then plunging downwards in a twisting flight.*

COOT *(right) The patch of pure white on the forehead has given it the nickname of 'bald coot'. It is an aggressive bird at all times, even towards its own species. Only two specimens of albino coot have ever been recorded at Hickling, amongst the thousands which have been shot.*

MARCH

1st

There are 4 adult Goldeneyes (males) on Hickling, 3 of them are in company with about 20 immatures. The largest and best male does not associate with these.

Saw quite 20 Shovelers, 8 of them being females.

Saw 4 Redshanks to-day.

2nd

Saw Lesser Spotted Woodpeckers in the Town Wood. There hundreds of Redwings roost in the alders. The Fieldfares generally roost on the marshes, amongst the sedge, there are some 30 or 40 roost amongst the sedge in front of Lodge.

HEN-HARRIER *A winter visitor to Hickling. It quarters the ground with great regularity for the small mammals, birds and reptiles which form its food. The flight is buoyant and frequently low; when flying, the white rump and lack of wing bars distinguish it clearly from the Montagu's harrier. The female is slightly larger and more brown above. This hawk is more widespread now in Britain than in 1911, thanks to its protection.*

3rd

The Bearded Tits are in good numbers again, so much so; that the reed cutters have noticed it, and remarked to me on the number of these birds all at once.

Nudd and I saw to-day what must have been a Common Buzzard against Sounds Plantation [*Heigham Woods*]. A Sparrowhawk was harassing it, and they went up a great height. It came gliding down, and flew away to Gibbs Wood. It looked about the size of a Short-eared Owl (longer tail) and flew like a Sparrowhawk. At first sight we thought it was a Rough-legged [*Buzzard*] when soaring, but could see it was not when it came closer.

4th

Saw 20 Widgeon and 3 Pintails, 2 males and a female.

5th

Saw 3 Great Crested Grebes, 7 Tufted Ducks, 2 Scaups, and about 15 Pochard on Heigham Sounds.

Saw 10 Redshanks in one flock.

6th

Saw 7 Common Teal in the War-bush, 3 adult Goldeneyes, 10 Widgeon (4 males), about 30 Pochard and 20 Tufted Ducks on Hickling Broad.

There were about 20 Redshanks and several Snipe, including some Jacks [*Jack Snipe*] on Deary's Marsh.

7th

The Redshanks are coming in, and Peewits are choosing their nesting sites. It is amusing to see Hoodies [*Hooded Crows*], Crows and Rooks get hustled by these birds on a marsh, to be hustled again by fresh birds on another one further one.

8th

Saw 2 pairs of Shovelers on Heigham Sounds, these no doubt are birds intending to stay.

I tried a rough count with the Coots on Hickling, and estimate their numbers at 1,700 or 1,800.

Saw a male Hen-harrier to-day, have not seen the female recently.

9th

A Hawfinch was brought to me that had been shot by a gardener. Should say it was a female.

19th

Saw 2 Ringed Plovers on Deary's Marsh in company with Redshanks.

20th

Wind N. Bitterly cold.

There are only 4 immature Goldeneyes on Hickling now.

Saw about 20 Pochard and 13 Tufted Ducks on Heigham Sounds, and one pair of Shovelers.

There are two pairs of Great Crested Grebes on the Sounds.

21st

There are an unusual number of Blackbirds about. I counted 60 on one field (ploughed) and 48 on an adjoining meadow.

22nd

The Bearded Tits have been very showy to-day, flying up in the air chasing each other, and pitching down into the reed beds. The males fighting for possession of females with tails outspread.

RINGED PLOVER *(with 3 redshanks) Sometimes called the 'ringed dotterel'. It breeds regularly on the coast of East Anglia, and can be distinguished from the rarer little ringed plover by the white on the forehead and broad eye stripe.*

REDSHANK *Breeds in the British Isles and as far north as Iceland. A sociable bird except when breeding, it has a shrill cry which is heard a long way off. Its food consists of aquatic insects, worms and small molluscs. Belongs to the same family – that of sandpipers – as the ringed plover.*

Saw a Snipe's nest that my father found in Mr Cotton's ground with 3 eggs. This is the earliest I've ever known.

—— 23rd ——

There are great number of Tits about, especially Long-tails and Marsh; Golden-crested Wrens are very much in evidence along the hedgerows and in the woods. I saw 2 working in a privet fence at breakfast time close to the window, well about 5 feet away, and am quite satisfied in myself they were two Fire-crested Wrens [Firecrests]. The stripe over the eye was clearly visible, and there looked to be a light band across the forehead at the base of the upper mandible. I looked at two or three Golden-crested during the day and could not see any of them were marked like the two I saw in the morning. I could see no perceptible difference in colour of the crests.

SHOVELER *(a pair) Known as a 'spoonbill' because of the shape of the bill, adapted for surface feeding; it dabbles for grass, worms, snails, aquatic insects and small crustacea. Resident throughout most of Britain, although breeding is restricted to areas like Hickling with suitable marshland. It is a fairly silent bird except when courting.*

TEAL *(3 pairs) The smallest British duck, and resident all year; in winter, its numbers are increased by visitors from Iceland and northern Europe. Often flies in compact flocks, and is a very sociable bird. Reacts quickly to danger, taking off almost vertically.*

—— 24th ——

There are hundreds of Fieldfares and Redwings about to-day.

Hoodies are congregating on the marshes, ready to take their departure. Shall not be sorry to lose them.

Saw a Barn Owl sitting in White Slea Wood, amongst the ivy overgrowing an alder tree.

—— 25th ——

Wind N.N.E. Strong wind and snow storms.

Saw a pair of Pintails on Hickling Broad, 3 Scaups, and a parcel of 7 Tufted Ducks.

—— 26th ——

Saw 3 pairs of Common Teal and a pair of Shovelers in Ball's Corner.

—— 27th ——

The Peewits have left the marshes for the upland. There promise to be a good number of these to stay and breed.

In looking through the Heigham Woods to-day, I see some of the Woodpecker boxes have been chipped a good bit, by Woodpeckers I presume. Several Great Tits are taking possession of the boxes.

Saw a pair of Dabchicks on Heigham Sounds, one of them took to wing and flew about 100 yards.

⟨— 28th —⟩

Saw a female Hen-harrier, had heard of it being seen for 2 days in Horsey Brayden by some marshmen.

There are a great number of Moorhens about this year, and Water Rails seem by their noises to be fairly common.

⟨— 29th —⟩

Went on Sounds, saw 5 Great Crested Grebes, 13 Pochard, 3 Tufted Ducks, and old male Scaup in magnificent plumage which is not common with us. Such old males are not often seen.

Saw a female White Eye [*White-eyed Pochard*] on the upper portion, it was swimming about no more than 25 yards away.

⟨— 30th —⟩

Saw a pair of (or two) Shags on Hickling Broad. They had been fishing on the Broad some time, after which they flew off seaward.

There are more Great Crested Grebes on Hickling and Sounds this year than last. Saw one after fish just in front of Lodge to-day.

⟨— 31st —⟩

Saw a pair of Garganeys against the Lodge, by their actions they seem to have been the pair that had their young against the Lodge last autumn.

Saw a Coot's nest with 2 eggs.

There are several pairs of Bearded Tits about, but have not seen any attempting to nest, though it is time for them. It may be the cold E. winds which have kept them backwards.

SCAUP *(top) A winter visitor, this rather solitary duck associates mainly with its own species. It is silent except in the breeding season, when its harsh and discordant call is accompanied by a toss of the head. It dives for its food, which includes mussels and small crabs.*

MOORHEN *(bottom) Also known as the 'water-hen'. A common bird and, like the coot, very aggressive in defence of its territory. When alarmed, it can submerge all of its body underwater except for its beak. Its food consists of slugs, worms, grass and insects.*

APRIL

➡ 1st ➡

Saw a Reeve [*female Ruff*] in company with
  Redshanks on Deary's Marsh, also 3 Garganeys.
Saw 14 Siskins in a flock feeding in some alders.
Saw the female White Eye on Sounds at the same
  spot as Wednesday.

➡ 3rd ➡

Howling gale from N.N.W. with snow squalls.
The Peewits have come from the marshes on to
  the uplands for shelter.
There are great quantities of Snipe on the
  marshes.
Saw a flock of 6 Golden Plovers heading against
  the wind, they came so close, could see two of
  them had black breasts.
Saw 6 Ring Ouzels under the leeside of the Town
  Wood, they were in excellent plumage.

GARGANEY *(left, 3 males and a female) Also known as
the 'cricket teal' because of the chirping noise made by
migrating males. Rarely seen in groups.*

SISKIN *(right) A winter visitor to Hickling, although it
is starting to breed in the new afforested areas of East
Anglia. Has a sweet twittering song of various notes.*

4th

Saw a Long-eared Owl in Gibbs Wood, but have not been able to locate a nest yet.

5th

Gale from E. with heavy snow squalls.
Birds having been seeking shelter wherever possible.
Great numbers of Bramblings and Chaffinches about, also Long-tailed Tits and Treecreepers.
6 Great Tits, 4 Blue Tits and 2 Long-tails have been nearly all day after some suet and fat meat I put out for them under a shrub against my door.

6th

There are a good number of Mallard about. Seen 30 Common Teal, 2 pairs of Shovelers in War-bush, 3 Garganeys on Deary's Marsh. On Heigham Sounds 4 Garganeys feeding within 15 yards, also a pair of Shovelers, 6 Tufted Ducks and about 20 Pochard.
The weather has quite upset birds nesting.

LONG-TAILED TIT *(left)* *Resident and abundant. Its large and splendid oval nest is lined with lichen outside and feathers inside. It has a small opening on the top side.*

BEARDED TIT *(right, a pair)* *Greatly increased since 1911 as a breeding species. Its song can be imitated by tapping two bronze coins together. A tame bird, which has been known to sit on a hand placed near the nest.*

7th

Saw a female Garganey against Lodge.
Reeve on Deary's Marsh, also a Curlew.
Jack Snipe are still with us in fair numbers.

9th

Mallard · Shoveler · Teal (4) · Garganey (3) Pochard · White-eyed Pochard (1) · Tufted Duck Goldeneye · Widgeon · Great Crested Grebe Coot · Snipe · Redshank · Reeve (1) · Ringed Plover · Curlew · Golden Plover · Green Plover [*Lapwing, or Peewit*] · Water Rail · Lesser Black-backed Gull · Herring Gull · Common Gull Black-headed Gull · Heron · Kestrel · Carrion Crow · Hooded Crow · Rook · Jackdaw · Jay

WILLOW WARBLER *(top left) An abundant summer visitor whose merry song, consisting of a few often-repeated notes, may be heard in nearly every wood. It is also one of the few features that prevent its confusion with the closely-related chiffchaff.*

MARSH TIT *(top right) Not as common at Hickling as elsewhere in Britain. Partial to rivers and alder bushes growing on swampy ground.*

SEDGE WARBLER *(bottom left) A summer visitor, and a bird that is heard more than seen. Its song is loud and merry, and it is known to mimic the calls of other birds. Likes thick vegetation near water, not necessarily sedge.*

MEADOW PIPIT *(bottom right) The smallest and most abundant of the pipit family, sometimes known as a 'tit-lark'. Cuckoos frequently lay their eggs in its nest.*

Wood-pigeon · Stock Dove · Starling · Blackbird Thrush · Redwing · Meadow Pipit · Moorhen Robin · Stonechat · Skylark · Hedge Sparrow Reed Bunting · Corn Bunting · Blue Tit · Coal Tit Marsh Tit · Bearded Tit · Greenfinch · Sparrow Pied Wagtail · Wren.

<u>Doubtful</u>: Greater Black-backed Gull, Yellow Wagtail.

In the War-bush there is a Mute Swan's nest containing 6 eggs, one of which though normal in texture and colour was the size of a Duck's but nearly round.

Reeve was on Deary's Marsh. The White-eye on S. end of the Sounds. Garganey (4) flying past Lodge, and 3 on Sounds and again on Deary's Marsh. The male whilst on the wing made a mewing note rather like a reed scraping along the edge of the boat, 'Queek'.

10th

Strong wind from N.W.
Lord Lucas and Hon. E. S. Montagu went away.
Saw several small flocks of Dunlins and Ringed Plovers going E.
Several Treecreepers and Marsh Tits in the Woods.
Saw a Robin's nest on the ground like a Pipit's with one egg.

13th

Found Bearded Tit's nest with two eggs.

14th

Light breeze from S. Warm sunny day.

Saw a Willow Wren [*Willow Warbler*] against Lodge.

White Wagtail running about on grass in front of Lodge.

A Marsh Harrier was working reed beds around Sounds. It looked like a female, by its size and dark brown plumage.

15th

Saw the first Swallow of the year to-day.

Found a Bearded Tit's nest with 4 eggs. Three Coots with eggs.

Seen Yellow Buntings [*Yellowhammers*] and a Greenfinch building their nests.

WHITE WAGTAIL *(top) A resident throughout the British Isles, and easily confused with the pied wagtail, except that it has a grey rather than black back and rump. It is an expert catcher of winged insects, its main food.*

CUCKOO *(bottom) Named after the sound of the male's courtship song, which is taken to be a sign of coming summer. First birds usually arrive in the middle of April, to mate and lay their eggs in other birds' nests; it is the only British bird to use this means of raising its offspring. Favours the nests of meadow pipits, reed and sedge warblers, robins and pied wagtails. Eats mainly insects such as caterpillars, spiders and earthworms.*

19th

Found a Chaffinch's nest with 2 eggs. This is the earliest I've ever known of this bird here.

Watched a pair of Blue Tits against the Town Wood alight on a field where oats were just springing, and found they tore off green stem and took the heart out of the oat, leaving the husk. One of them took 6 or 7 oats, along the drill mark. First time I've noticed Tits feeding on corn. No doubt springing oats being sweet and of a fatty substance would just suit their palate.

20th

Saw and heard the Cuckoo for first time this year.

21st

Saw Sedge Warblers, and Whitethroats to-day.

Two Reeves on Deary's Marsh.

Saw a pair of Garganeys on the Big Rande.

23rd

CUCKOO SUCKING EGGS?

Mr Linkhorn (keeper) reports to me, when standing in the White Slea Wood not far from a Thrush's nest containing 4 eggs (which he previously knew of) a Cuckoo came and settled upon the edge of the nest and sucked the 4 eggs, throwing the egg-shells upon the ground after emptying the contents.

I do not doubt the accuracy of his statement, as I have found him to be very truthful.

The majority of the local people are imbued with the idea that eggs of other birds are the principal food of the Cuckoos. Personally have never seen a Cuckoo suck eggs, though I have found eggs sucked by a bird, but whether it has been the work of a Jay, have not been able to prove.

26th

Blue Tits building in nesting box against Lodge.
Bearded Tit's nest against Lodge, young just hatching.
Saw 2 Jack Snipe.

27th

Saw the Garganeys, which I believe are nesting same place as last year.
Nudd and I saw a Heron pounce down from a post on Heigham Sounds that marks the channel way into 4 feet of water, whether after a fish, or if it was having a quick bath, cannot say, but we have neither seen a Heron do such thing before, though we have seen scores at different times on these posts and on Hickling. It shook its feathers several times after returning to post.

28th

Saw the Marsh Harrier working about in the War-bush after Coots' eggs. It looked like a male, judging by its size, as it was a small bird and light brown.

29th

Saw an adult male Redstart this morning. These are rare with us in spring, commoner in the autumn.
Also saw a male Wheatear.
Saw 2 Fieldfares at Horsey and some Brambling Finches.

30th

Went on Heigham Sounds and saw what I took to be 2 Black-necked or Eared Grebes.
I know the Slavonian in spring and autumn dress and feel sure they were not these. One was in deep water and dived very similar to a Coot when feeding quietly. The other flew several yards on top of water and the white bars were very conspicuous.

JACK SNIPE *(top) A winter visitor, sometimes seen in flocks which are known as 'wisps'. Slightly smaller than the common snipe, hence its diminutive name, and also distinguished by two streaks on the crown compared to the larger snipe's one. Its food consists mainly of beetle larvae, snails and worms which it finds by probing in boggy terrain with its long bill.*

BLACK-NECKED GREBE *(bottom) A rare visitor from its breeding grounds in Europe and southern Russia, known locally as the 'eared grebe' because of its golden ear-tufts. Mainly solitary, though on occasion just a pair have been seen at Hickling, as here. Its food consists of fish, crustacea and water-beetles.*

MAY

⟢ 1st ⟣

Mr Linkhorn, the new keeper, reports to me seeing a bird circling round Deary's Marsh last night, and came over him about 80 yards up. By the description which was very good, should say it was a Spoonbill.
Saw the Marsh Harrier about.

⟢ 3rd ⟣

Saw a Lesser Whitethroat.
Several Grasshopper Warblers.

⟢ 4th ⟣

Saw 3 Ringed Plovers.
A boy showed me a Cuckoo's egg, taken from a Hedge Sparrow's nest.
Found 3 Redshanks' nests with 2 eggs in each, and a Snipe's nest with 3 eggs on the Big Rande.

SHOVELER *(left) See page 49.*

SKYLARK *(right, young bird) A resident of Britain, and in spring and summer a perpetual and delightful songster; it sings while on the ground, soars gracefully and descends, still singing. A sociable bird after the breeding season, often feeding in flocks.*

6th

Mr Russell came to-day. We looked for Black-necked Grebes but saw nothing of them.
Saw White-eyed Pochard, 2 male Tufted Ducks, 2 male Pochards and Crested Grebes on Sounds.

7th

Mr Russell and I saw Reeve on Deary's Marsh and male Shoveler.
Spotted Shank flying over Big Rande.
Marsh Harrier on Heigham Sounds.

8th

Saw an immature male Montagu's Harrier. It is one of the poorest in plumage I've ever seen, not much grey showing.
Saw 2 Grey Plovers, and 4 Knots going in a N.E. direction about 30 yards high when on Hickling Broad.

9th

Have seen to-day an old male Montagu and a female. These may be the pair that bred last year, as the male was not in good plumage and would have improved in plumage this year, but of this it is difficult to prove.

10th

Found 2 Bearded Tits' nests with 6 eggs and 5 young ones on Heigham Sounds, and one in White Slea with young.

Alfred Nudd reports seeing a male Pintail in the War-bush.

11th

Heard and saw the Nightingale warbling away in the Town Wood. I went and listened to it about 10 p.m. It is seldom heard in this locality. I heard one some years ago in Gibbs Wood, and flushed bird from nest containing 5 eggs.
There are several Garden Warblers in the Woods.
Saw the Pintail in War-bush. It is in excellent plumage.

12th

Found 4 Bearded Tits' nests on Heigham Sounds, 2 with 7 and 6 eggs, 2 with young ones.
Saw a Greenshank on Deary's Marsh.
The female Montagu came past close to Lodge this morning, and the male was working on the marshes at the back in the evening.

MONTAGU'S HARRIER *A spring and summer visitor from Africa and southern Europe. The smallest of the harrier family, it was identified by Col. George Montagu, a nineteenth-century Devon naturalist. The story of its discovery as a breeding species in 1910 in Hickling is told in the introduction to this book. A male Montagu's harrier has been known to be polygamous at Hickling, with three females nesting. Like all the harrier family, it is a most graceful bird in flight. Its food consists mainly of small birds, mammals, snakes and some insects.*

13th

A Black-tailed Godwit came past me when on Heigham Sounds about 4 a.m. flying in an easterly direction about 20 yards high.

Saw the Swifts for first time this spring.

There is a decided increase in Reed Warblers to-day.

Saw Sedge Warbler's nest with 2 eggs.

Have seen nothing whatever this week of the Black-necked Grebes, and think they must have moved on.

14th

Wind E. veering to S. Light breeze, rained all day without a break.

NIGHTINGALE *(top left)* *A rare spring and summer visitor to Hickling. The song can be heard by day and night, but ceases after the young are born in June.*

KNOT *(top right)* *May be named after King Canute, because it loves the edge of the sea, or its call, 'knut, knut'. Flocks abound on the sandbanks and estuaries of the east coast between early autumn and late spring.*

WHITE-WINGED BLACK TERN *(bottom left)* *A rare visitor to Hickling, often found with the more common black tern. The feathers on the forewing, rump and tail do not become white until the third year.*

LITTLE TERN *(bottom right)* *Smallest and rarest of the tern family, appearing on Britain's eastern coasts in May to nest in colonies on sand and shingle beaches. It does not show fear during the nesting period if disturbed.*

Saw 2 White-winged Black Terns in company with 8 Black Terns against Tent Hill. They came so close as I was lying in amongst reeds, could see their red beaks and legs. The white on the shoulders of wings and the white tail and rump made the black look intenser than on the Black Terns.

Could see they were White-winged Black Terns 200 yards away, as there was a black cloud in the background which made them look very conspicuous at a distance, and easily distinguishable from the Black Terns.

It was a great treat for me to watch them. After watching them within 10 yards of me very often, I reluctantly came away amidst a downpour of rain, after spending the best hour this spring.

16th

Calm hot day.

Saw a Pied Flycatcher against Lodge (female).

2 Black Terns flying about on White Slea.

Watched Harriers (Montagu's) at Horsey Brayden, both birds which appear to be settling down for nesting.

17th

DUCK'S EGGS EXPOSED 22 HOURS

A remarkable incident came under my notice, and think it worth recording to show how long ducks can remain from their eggs without any serious harm coming to the young in the shell.

A lady walking along the wall [*round Hickling Broad*] with a dog came across one of our decoys [*a duck with clipped wings, used to attract passing ducks to the area*] sitting upon eggs which the dog promptly killed. This was on Monday morning last at 11 a.m., and I did not know of the affair until after 8 o'clock yesterday morning (Tuesday) when I sent Linkhorn to get the eggs; therefore it was 9 a.m. before the eggs were taken up, brought home and put under a hen, and this morning 9 young ducks have hatched out of the 11 eggs, the remaining 2 being dead birds. Thus making 22 hours at least the eggs were uncovered.

I knew of Water Rail that was kept off her eggs 10 hours and hatched out alright. This was 6 days previous to the hatching out.

19th

Saw young Skylarks that flew from nest a short distance.

The male Montagu came by Lodge this afternoon. I think they will very soon nest.

MALLARD (*female*) *Less common locally than it used to be, owing to the progress of drainage schemes. There are still a few places where decoys are worked with profit. The nest, made of grass and lined with down, is usually on the ground near to water and sometimes in a hollow tree. The young take to the water soon after the last egg is hatched.*

20th

The male and female Montagus have been spending the greater part of to-day on the marsh at the back of White Slea. They have been calling to each other, and by their movements they may even nest on this marsh within 200 yards of Lodge.

A pair of Flycatchers (Spotted) are around the Lodge.

22nd

The pair of Montagus have commenced sleeping on the marsh at back of Lodge.

Saw 2 Common Sandpipers this morning sitting on quay heading dressing themselves.

Found a Sedge Warbler's nest with 6 eggs.

Found a Grasshopper Warbler in nest not far from Lodge, 5 eggs.

23rd

Wind E. Heavy dew in morning.

Went to Horsey Brayden and saw the pair of Montagus there, the female carried some material to one or two places as if intending to build.

Saw a Lesser [*Little*] Tern on Hickling Broad.

24th

When the male or female Montagu works over this ground the Redshanks gather around them. Have seen 25 or 30 around them at once.

25th

Saw 3 young Great Crested Grebes on Heigham Sounds. They were thrown from the back of parent bird as she dived for the thick reeds at edge of roadway.

Alfred Nudd found a Great Crested Grebe's nest with one egg when cutting a roadway through a reed bed.

Saw 2 Ringed Plovers in the War-bush.

The Montagu (female) carried some material for nesting this morning against Lodge.

26th

The Montagus against Lodge have not got eggs yet but think the female has found the right nesting spot, as she has been carrying more material to this place than the others.

Found a Goldfinch's nest with young just hatching in the carpenter's garden, Hickling. The nest is placed in a pear tree. This is the first Goldfinch's nest I've ever found in the village.

27th

About 2 p.m. this afternoon when Linkhorn and myself were cutting rushes by the edge of Pleasure Hill, an adult Spoonbill came flying from the War-bush way. It was about 25 yards high and 60 yards off. It made several circles in the air rising higher every time until 70 yards high, when it flew straight off due E. Could see the gleaming white plumage away to Horsey.

Saw a Knot in red dress [*its summer plumage*] come past and alight with Redshanks on the Big Rande. It allowed me to approach within 20 yards of it and quietly flew round and settled behind me when I came away and left it; as it flew by, it kept uttering a low chuck-chuck, chuck-chuck.

28th

Saw the female Garganey on Heigham Sounds with 8 young ones, they looked to be very small, probably 3 or 4 days old. The old female was very fussy and tried to draw me away, feigning lameness.

30th

Saw the female Montagu building in a new place on the marsh at back of White Slea. Do not think there are any eggs yet.

Saw a Reeve on Deary's Marsh. Whether it is the one that frequented this place some time ago, cannot say; I watched it but it gave no clue as nesting bird, for it was there at least 3 hours, and if it was nesting would have returned to its nest before then.

MONTAGU'S HARRIER *(female) Like all birds of prey, the female is larger than the male. The nest is composed of rushes, sedge or coarse grasses lined with finer materials, made on an open piece of ground surrounded by high vegetation. Both sexes take part in building but the female does most of the work.*

JUNE

⟶ 1st ⟵

Looked at Harrier's nest for first time against Lodge when the female was off. It contained one egg. There was very little material for a nest, could easily have held the lot in one hand. I think the female does the larger share of building after the first egg is laid.

⟶ 2nd ⟵

Saw the female go to her nest against Lodge, but have seen nothing of the male all day.

Went to Horsey and saw a pair of Montagu's Harriers against Blackfleet, and 2 more pairs on Horsey Brayden, also a Marsh Harrier which came very close to me.

The 2 pairs of Montagus came in only Thursday or Wednesday the latest. Thus making 4 pairs of Montagu's Harriers in the neighbourhood.

SPARROWHAWK *Fairly common at Hickling, and on the increase throughout Britain since it became a protected species in 1966. Preys mainly on small birds, including sparrows, finches and game-bird chicks. Lays about five eggs, usually in May, in a nest of twigs built in a tree; the female does most if not all of the building, and all the incubation.*

Saw a Coot chase a female Pochard (wounded bird). It dived after it and seized the Pochard by its head. The Pochard seemed quite dazed after such an attack, scarcely knowing which way to go.

⟶ 3rd ⟵

Lord Lucas came this afternoon.

We saw Montagu's nest against Lodge with 2 eggs and both birds.

⟶ 4th ⟵

Lord Lucas and myself went to War-bush early, saw Mallard in eclipse plumage, Knot in red dress, and a Ringed Plover. Saw Ruff on Deary's Marsh and Big Rande.

Went to Horsey, saw a Montagu's nest against Blackfleet ready for eggs. Saw another pair in Brayden settling for nesting.

I saw the Marsh Harrier.

⟶ 5th ⟵

Lord Lucas and myself went to the War-bush before breakfast. Saw Common Teal, Ringed Plover, Dunlin with black breast.

Looked at Harrier's nest against Lodge, it contained three eggs.

One against Blackfleet, one egg.

Found one in Horsey Brayden with three eggs.

8th

Looked at Harrier's nest against Lodge, and the one in Horsey Brayden. These two contained 4 eggs in each.

One at Blackfleet contained 2 eggs.

My father told me this morning as he was coming down White Slea wall he saw a male Montagu knock down a young Pheasant that flew across a dyke. The remainder of the brood hid in a bush.

9th

Found a Snipe (Common) nest with 2 eggs on the Big Rande. The eggs are the smallest I've ever seen, and if I had not flushed the bird from nest, should have been obliged to visit the nest again to see if it was a Jack Snipe's, as I have seen a Jack on this rande recently.

DUNLIN *(top) Known locally as the 'sea snipe'. The commonest of all shore birds, and one of the smallest; sometimes flocks on estuaries can number hundreds. It is distinguished in summer by its black belly.*

BLACK TERN *(bottom) An irregular summer visitor to Britain, probably due to the drainage of swampy land suitable for nesting: eggs were last taken in Norfolk in 1858.*

10th

Saw the two Garganey ducks together on the sounds. They both seem to have got young.

Saw a remarkable light specimen of the Common Heron. Have heard of it being seen by marshmen several times.

11th

Found the fourth Montagu's nest in Horsey Brayden with two eggs.

13th

Saw a Black Tern (good bird) on Hickling Broad.

Saw 9 Geese flying away W. about 20 yards high. They looked like Egyptians. These often occur in the summer months. No doubt escaped birds from somewhere.

Have seen nothing whatever of the male Montagu against Lodge and have great fears he is dead. The watchers in Horsey Brayden report not having seen their male since Monday morning. But the female has been off after food 3 or 4 times. Seldom remaining away more than 20 minutes.

14th

Gale from the N.N.W. Very cold.

Have seen 8 Lesser, 2 Common, and 2 Black Terns to-day.

Sailed quite close to a Grey Phalarope on Hickling. Did not notice it until within 10 yards of it, owing to heavy swell. It took to wind and flew away to the War-bush.

Saw the female Montagu go off the nest after food.

15th

Have seen nothing whatever of the female against Lodge. Went to nest after dinner. Eggs cold.

Went off to Horsey Brayden, and found the watchers had seen nothing whatever of their female since last night 6 p.m. when she went off to feed. Looked at their eggs and found they were quite cold.

Was obliged to take up at dusk these two clutches of 4 eggs each of the Harriers, and shift the watchers to the other nest in Brayden.

Both birds of this nest and the one at Blackfleet are still safe.

I think that some malicious person or persons are either shooting or trapping them, probably the latter, and as these birds range so far after food it is difficult to find out who.

16th

None of the watchers have seen any odd Harriers about to-day, only the respective pairs belonging to each nest. Therefore am led to believe the other two pairs are dead.

Saw Pied Wagtail building.

19th

Saw a young Cuckoo that could fly remarkably well. This is the first I've seen this year. The foster parents were Yellow Wagtails.

Snipe continue to drum.

There is a male Shoveler on Sounds in eclipse plumage. They generally leave us in end of May.

20th

Wind S.W. Thunderstorms, heavy showers.

Owing to the water rising was obliged to hoist the nest of Montagu's Harrier near Blackfleet by putting material under the foundations of nest. The nest is composed of very little material. It is one of the barest I've seen.

Saw 2 Curlews, and a Green Sandpiper on Hickling.

GREY PHALAROPE *(top) Normally a winter visitor; much rarer in spring. Seen here in winter plumage; in summer, the neck and underparts are reddish-brown. The phalarope family are very tame and will allow observation at close quarters. They swim on the water like miniature gulls, darting here and there for insects. The males are slightly smaller than the females.*

PIED WAGTAIL *(bottom) First distinguished from the white wagtail on the Continent in 1820. Usually two broods are reared in a season. The nest is made of grass and roots, lined with hair and feathers, and is built in the cleft of a wall, a decayed tree, the thatching of a building, or sometimes in an open field.*

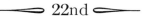

22nd

CORONATION OF KING GEORGE V

Saw a Swift on Hickling Broad when crossing over
to the village for Coronation festivities, with a
piece of red tape tied on to its leg.

Hon. E. S. Montagu came this evening.

23rd

Looked at both Harriers' nests which contained
three eggs each.

Saw both pairs of Montagus.

25th

Mr Russell, friend, and myself saw Sparrowhawk
go from her nest in Gibbs Wood.

Snipe still drumming, and Cuckoos calling.

26th

We saw both males of Montagus bring food, and
the females go up and take it.

Mr Russell and friend found a Lesser Redpoll's
nest with 5 eggs in White Slea Wood.

Lord Lucas, Miss Herbert and Mr Argles arrived
this evening.

GREEN SANDPIPER *Not uncommon in the spring and
autumn migration. Usually found alone or in pairs on
peaty swamps and near fresh water, rarely in a family
party. Its flight is rapid and erratic, and when alarmed
it gives a shrill cry. It uses its beak to probe for insects,
worms and molluscs.*

JUNE

27th

Lord Lucas and Miss Herbert saw both Montagus'
nests and both males feed the females.
Found Yellow Wagtail's nest with 5 eggs.
Saw a Green Sandpiper flying over White Slea.

28th

Saw an adult Black Tern on Hickling Broad. This
is very late.

29th

Went to Royal Show.
Overheard an old man who was looking at a new
motor boat with awning over, say to another:
'You wouldn't catch me ever going up in one of
them things,' thinking no doubt it was a flying
machine.

30th

A Reeve came flying past the Lodge, going on to
Hickling Broad.
There are quite 3,000 Starlings come to sleep on
the reeds in the War-bush. They have come in
earlier this year, and in greater numbers.

STARLING *Best known for its song, imitative powers
and habit of congregating in large flocks at roosting
times, even in cities. The large resident population is
joined in the autumn by flocks arriving on Britain's
eastern coasts; in winter, huge flocks roosting at night in
reed beds can do much damage.*

JULY

4th

Young one in Montagu's nest near Blackfleet this
  morning.
Several Curlews about.

5th

There are several Great Crested Grebes which
  have come off well with their young.
Found a Corn Bunting's nest.

6th

Saw a Common Scoter on Heigham Sounds. It
  looked in good condition and flew strong.
Looked at Montagus near Blackfleet; there were 2
  young ones, the other egg just hatching.

BITTERN *The story of the rediscovery of this secretive
bird as a breeding species near Hickling is told in the
introduction to this book, and in the diary itself. Since
then, it has spread to neighbouring counties, but appears
over the last few years to be on the decline again at
Hickling. A solitary bird, it avoids danger by freezing
with its beak pointed skywards, blending in shape and
colour with the reeds surrounding it. The nest, placed on
swampy ground, is made of rushes, and there are usually
four to six eggs.*

7th

Light breeze from W. Very hot.
Have heard the last few days of Bittern (Common)
  being seen at Sutton 2 miles from Hickling. Miss
  Turner and myself asked Mr Robert Gurney,
  whose ground they were on, about them. He
  stated he had never seen the bird, but his keeper
  had, and he gave us permission to go and hunt
  for them. We arrived about 1.30 p.m., and after
  waiting some time the bird crossed us, and after
  flying at least 500 yards. An hour after it
  returned again, about the same time back it
  came to the same place. We moved to a position
  abreast of it, and saw the bird get up and flop
  above the reeds a few yards. I dived off for a 100
  yards into a thick bed of reeds and gladden [*local
  name for a species of reed*], principally gladden,
  up to my thighs of mud and water, and could see
  where the new gladden was broken, no doubt by
  the old Bittern clutching it upon alighting. When
  close to where she alighted, heard her quarking
  away, and flushed her about 5 yards away when
  she became very noisy and fussy; I searched
  round, but could see or find nothing whatever.

After tea Miss Turner and myself went back, and
both went upon my old track, heard the bird
talking away and flushed her ahead. I searched
round where she got up and found a young one,
beak and neck skywards. He was two-thirds
grown. Could hardly realize it.

8th

Saw a Spotted Shank in the War-bush.
Went with Miss Turner at 3 a.m., found young
Bittern and he was photographed in various
attitudes.
Saw the old bird fly across the reeds twice, and
first time of entering the high reeds walked
within 10 yards of it, but was guided by the bird
uttering its quark, quark, could find no nest, or
any other youngsters though I have not the least
doubt there are some others, but as it is
impossible to see one's way cannot systematically work the ground, and the young could very
easily be passed.

SPOTTED REDSHANK *(left, top)* *An irregular visitor to*
Hickling. Lacks the common redshank's wing bars.
When flushed, it flies around uttering a shrill cry.

WHIMBREL *(left, bottom)* *Also known as the 'seven*
whistlers', after its repeated whistling call. A bird of the
sea shore, not common at Hickling.

CORN BUNTING *(right)* *Not common at Hickling. The*
flight is heavy, the legs hanging down at first as if
broken. The male's song is rather harsh and monotonous.

10th

Two young Sparrowhawks flew out of nest in Gibbs Wood when I stood below and gave the tree a shake.

11th

Looked at Montagu's Harriers near Blackfleet, the male brought an unfledged skylark.

12th

Saw some young Corn Buntings just ready to leave nest.

Man cutting marsh near the Town Wood found a Nightjar's nest with one egg.

Saw 3 Dunlins on the edge of Pleasure Island. The water is very low so that the edges of randes etc. are quite bare, 6 or 8 feet being ideal now for waders. The Snipe and young Plover with an occasional Redshank frequent these edges a great deal.

13th

Looked at young Montagus near Blackfleet and took some food (Sparrows) and a Moorhen pulled in pieces, as the old male was not seen once yesterday, so that the old female had to hunt.

I heard towards evening the male turned up about 12 noon having been away about 40 hours. He brought a young Yellow Wag [Wagtail].

Both males are feeding very slow this year in comparison with last year's male.

The young at this nest have turned buff colour.

The watcher said the female and young cleared up the Moorhen and Sparrows.

14th

Wind N. Misty evening.

Saw a Whimbrel and a Greenshank on the mud in the War [-bush], also Mallard, Shoveler and Common Teal.

Found a Yellow Wag's nest on the Big Rande with eggs, the bird is sitting.

15th

The Great Crested Grebes are flying about a great deal now. Have noticed they generally do at this time of year. These are old birds. Whether it is to show the young how they should do it, or it may be the migratory instinct is asserting itself, thus causing them to be more restless.

Young Pied and Yellow Wags are daily catching flies on the grass in front of Lodge.

17th

Saw a Red-legged Partridge still sitting.

GREAT CRESTED GREBE *Has greatly increased in number during this century, due to its protection. The nest is usually a mass of aquatic plants floating on the water's surface. Both parents guard the young which are sometimes carried on the adults' backs, just forward of the wings.*

18th

Saw 11 Garganey, and 15 Common Teal came wheeling around against White Slea. Some of these frequent the War-bush.

Was asked to go and help to find the Bittern's nest at Sutton. Miss Turner, Rev. Bird [*a local collector*], Robert Gurney Esq., his keeper and myself. We systematically worked the thick reed and found the nest not far from where I found the young one. The foundation of nest was of old dead gladden stems, the lining of nest consisting entirely of dead reeds that were very rotten.

Some downy small feathers were adhering to nest, and was covered with mealy or scaly stuff from the youngsters. Was surprised not to see any white-wash or dung round the nest similar to the Herons'.

20th

Saw a Grasshopper Warbler's nest with 2 fresh eggs, that was cut up by a marshman.

Saw the male Garganey, there is the grey colour on the shoulders of his wing that is still visible in flight though he is in eclipse plumage.

GREENSHANK *A regular visitor, though in small numbers, and there are no records of nesting at Hickling. It has a strong and rapid flight, and when disturbed it utters a loud cry. Its food consists mainly of small fish and spawn, worms and insects.*

21st

Saw and heard a Snipe drumming. This is very late. There are quite a good number of Snipe on the marshes, frequenting where it is wet and shady.

22nd

Mosquitoes are awfully trying at nights.

Saw 2 Green Sandpipers and a Ringed Plover.

A good number of Mallard may be seen moving about in the mornings and evenings now.

23rd

Saw a Greenshank when crossing Hickling Broad.

24th

About 9 a.m. when up the Look-out [*at White Slea Lodge*], saw a Pintail come flying past Lodge unto the Broad (Hickling). Whether male or female could not say, but was absolutely certain as to species, as it was within 60 yards. Have never seen a Pintail during the summer months, but Gadwalls occasionally occur in July and August.

Saw a Yellowhammer's nest with 2 fresh eggs.

26th

Calm morning. Heavy rain and thunderstorms.

Several parcels of Snipe were on the move before the storm, or signs of it in the morning.

Saw an immature Black Tern on Hickling early.
 (Brayden) watcher reports the male Montagu
 took 3 lots of food in 45 minutes, and was not
 seen for several hours.

⟾ 28th ⟾

The watcher in Brayden came and reported the
 loss of young Montagus, which would have flown
 in 10 or 12 days. Went to look, and found an
 otter had been, and found one young amongst
 the thick sedge with its head badly bitten, and
 half one wing eaten off.
Have placed 2 traps each side of the young one.
The watcher's suspicions were aroused by the
 female going to nest, wheeling away and
 screaming.
[*Jimmy*] Peggs, the Horsey keeper, saw an otter
 on this marsh only on Wednesday and knocked
 the young one that was with it on the head with
 his punt pole, he tried to get the old one but
 failed.

GRASSHOPPER WARBLER *A summer visitor which
owes its name to its rapid trilling song which resembles
the chirping of some grasshoppers. Sometimes called the
'reeler' as the song also sounds like a fishing reel running
out with the ratchet on. Although not plentiful, it seems
rarer than it is, owing to its skulking habits. The nest is
one of the most elusive to find as, built in thick vegetation,
it is often reached by a tunnel, the mouth of which can be
ten to fifteen yards from the actual nest.*

30th

Wind S. dropping to calm.

Saw **5 Wood Sandpipers** on the mud in the War-bush. They flew up and returned soon after, and within 20 yards of me. They run very close to the Green Sandpiper, but for their note would be easily overlooked.

Saw a Reeve on the Big Rande.

31st

After a shower this morning I saw upon a dead bush overhanging the reeds growing in the dyke at back of Lodge: 2 Bearded Tits, 2 Sedge Warblers, 1 Reed Warbler, 1 Blue Tit, 1 Pied Wagtail, 1 House Sparrow. These 6 species were sitting in a space of 4 feet preening and drying themselves.

It is uncommon to see Bearded Tits sitting upon bushes, though it may not be unusual for them where there are bushes and small trees growing in close proximity to reeds.

REED WARBLER *A summer visitor with a long and varied song which is heard during the day but best of all at twilight; it has also been known to mimic other birds. The nest is built, mainly by the female, of grasses woven around about four growing reeds which strengthen and support it, so that in a strong wind the eggs will not roll out. This small bird is one of the cuckoo's favourite victims. As its name suggests, it is usually seen hopping about reed beds. Its food consists of marsh insects, spiders, slugs and worms.*

AUGUST

Light breeze from S. Very hot.

Lord Lucas and the Hon. E. S. Montagu were out early this morning for duck. We saw during the day, Mallard, Shovelers, Tufted Duck, Garganey and Common Teal, 2 Spotted Shanks, Wood Sandpipers, Little Stint, Common Sandpiper, and Dunlin with black breast.

Saw a great number of Bearded Tits on Heigham Sounds.

⟹ 2nd ⟹

I saw a Long-eared Owl at back of Lodge sitting on the bush watching for the birds that were roosting in the reeds to come forth. This was 3.30 a.m.

WOOD SANDPIPER *(left) An uncommon visitor to Norfolk, usually in the autumn. There is no record of a nest at Hickling. Smaller than the green sandpiper. Its food consists of worms, small molluscs and insects.*

JAY *(right) Common in most British woodlands, and notorious for its raids on other birds' nests for their eggs and young. Also eats worms, berries, acorns and beechmast, which are no problem for its powerful bill.*

3rd

A pair of Nightjars were hawking round the bushes against Lodge at dusk.

4th

Two of the three young Montagu's Harriers can fly about.

5th

This evening Miss Turner and myself saw 96 Common Terns come over White Slea Lodge going W. about 50 yards high. Have never seen so many at one time apart from their nesting ground, or upon tidal water.

Saw a Reed Bunting's nest in the War marshes with 3 young about a week old.

A man cut up a Grasshopper Warbler's nest with 3 fresh eggs.

8th

Lowne of Yarmouth [*a taxidermist*] showed me a male Montagu received from Martham, that was shot and sent to him. It no doubt is the male from near Blackfleet, as he has been missing the last few days, and corresponds with him in plumage. The place where it was shot is about $1\frac{1}{2}$ to 2 miles as the crow flies.

11th

The female Montagu and the 3 young ones were flying about down Meadow Dyke.

12th

Saw a Greenshank on the mud in War-bush. It came several times within 10 yards as I lay concealed amongst the reeds.

It seemed to be feeding principally upon insects, being very quick in its movements, but ever on the alert.

14th

Saw a Marsh Harrier working the reed beds on Heigham Sounds. It is a very dark specimen, the creamy head being visible.

15th

Little Stint and a Common Sandpiper on the mud in the War-bush.

NIGHTJAR *Not common at Hickling because of the lack of plantations, and decreasing elsewhere in Britain. Named after its nocturnal habits and 'churring' song. Lives entirely on insects which it takes on the wing in twilight and on moonlit nights. Sometimes referred to as the 'goatsucker' in the mistaken belief that it frequents grazing pastures to milk the animals rather than to catch the flies they attract. Unlike other birds, who sit crossways on a branch, the nightjar sits lengthways with the head lower than the tail.*

⟾ 16th ⟽

Saw the 3 young Montagus near Blackfleet on my way to Horsey. They have shorter tails than the old bird, and look the colour of a Marsh Harrier.

⟾ 17th ⟽

Saw the Marsh Harrier on White Slea.
Sand Martins and Swallows are roosting in the reeds by thousands on Hickling and Heigham Sounds at night. Saw a Sand Martin with white tail, rump and back amongst them.

HERON *(left) Known locally as an 'old harnser'. Except for the breeding season, it is often solitary and shy, like its close relative, the bittern. The alarm note is very loud and can be heard some distance away. Its food consists mainly of small fish, frogs, water-voles and other small mammals, which it stabs with its sharp bill.*

MARSH HARRIER *(right) The largest of the harrier family, arriving in the spring. In 1915 it nested at Hickling after an absence of twenty-seven years, and successfully raised four young. Since that time it has returned almost every year, although it is still a rare breeder and is once again on the decline. Nest is composed of water-plants lined with grasses, hidden in thick marsh vegetation. Its food consists of coots, moorhens and other birds, their eggs and young, snakes, frogs and water-voles.*

19th

Wind S.E. Thunderstorms in evening (rain).

Caught a Reed Warbler in the boat house, whose feet, beak and feathers were covered with spiders' webs that made it impossible to fly far. These webs were adhering to the feet and beak as large as little nuts, and had matted the tail and wing feathers together. It must have been in this state for 2 or 3 days as the bird was thin and wasted.

After giving it a good clean-up it flew away amongst the bushes apparently quite happy, and commenced to feed ravenously on the insects.

My father and I heard a Bittern calling several times at dusk on this end of Sounds. My father stated he saw it fly from White Slea to the Sounds early Friday morning, when he was after his eel net.

Saw the Marsh Harrier on Deary's Marsh.

20th

Linkhorn states he saw the female Montagu take a good-sized young Partridge to-day, and take it to the 3 young ones that were flying about on the Meadows.

21st

Wind S. Clear warm day.

A man mowing round a barley field cut into a Hen Pheasant sitting upon 9 eggs.

Saw 10 Jays at Gibbs Wood, also Sparrowhawks and Kestrel.

Willow Wrens, Whitethroats and Reed Warblers were after insects amongst the trees.

22nd

Saw quite a number of Yellow Wags on Pleasure Hill, probably a batch that were resting on their way S.

Several young Cuckoos frequent bushes around Lodge.

There are a good number of family parties of Curlews passing. Two companies of 8 and 7 rested on Pleasure Island until disturbed by passing early boats.

23rd

Saw the Marsh Harrier flying over White Slea.

Several waders are going S. to-day, principally Dunlins and Ringed Plovers.

Saw 5 Bar-tailed Godwits which would have settled on Pleasure [*Island*], but for a boat with a fisherman in they did not like.

BAR-TAILED GODWIT *A regular visitor to Britain's estuaries in the spring and autumn migration, shown here in its winter dress; in summer, the head, neck and underparts are chestnut-red, the mantle wood-brown and black, the rump white with dark streaks. Seldom seen inland, usually found in flocks on the seashore together with other shore birds, such as the knot.*

24th

A Kingfisher this morning came and perched on one of the mooring stakes along side the quay heading, from which he dived in and returned with a small roach or rudd.

Swallows are feeding their second brood in the boat shed.

25th

Several Herons roost in Sounds and Gibbs Woods.

The Sand Martins with a few House Martins and Swallows amongst them are streaming from one Broad to another in thousands. At times they mount up until they look like specks, or like a flight of bees, and then swoop down again with lightning rapidity.

No doubt this means they will soon be going.

SPOTTED CRAKE *(top) An uncommon, mostly non-breeding summer visitor, difficult to observe because of its skulking habits and preference for swamps and marshes.*

LITTLE STINT *(bottom) Arrives each year on its autumn migration. Fairly numerous on the seashore, but rare inland. Resembles a miniature dunlin but lacks the black breast. When roused, it gives off a low clicking noise; in a large flock they sound like chirping grasshoppers.*

26th

Saw a Ruff and 4 Reeves on Wet Spurlings [*Meadow Dyke*].

Saw a Gadwall on the Sounds in company with 2 Shovelers.

The bulk of the Martins are gone.

27th

Saw female Montagu flying over Sounds with food.

28th

Flushed a Spotted Crake on Deary's Marsh, and have put up 2 Land Rails to-day.

Heard the Bittern calling about 8 p.m. as it was flying towards Hickling.

31st

Calm day, very hot.

Saw 3 Avocets sitting on Pleasure Island at 5.30 this morning. They were sleeping, and as I punted by, they raised their heads and paid no attention to me whatever though I was within 40 yards of them.

When I returned from War-bush an hour later, they were gone.

SEPTEMBER

1st

Looked over ground at Potter Heigham, and saw over 100 Partridges. Coveys are good and strong, but shy owing to not much cover in the roots.

4th

Saw a Robin at Hickling with pure white wings and tail, the other part was of the usual colour. It looked extremely handsome with this partial change of plumage.

ENGLISH PARTRIDGE *(left) Abundant in Norfolk. Over the last fifty years many thousands have been keeper-reared, so that the early strains may no longer be recognized. Both parents guard their young from birth until maturity, and they live as a family, known as a covey.*

ROBIN *(right) Also known as the 'redbreast', and Britain's national bird. Often very tame, unlike its Continental cousin. A solitary bird, vigorous and even pugnacious in defence of its territory. Albino, grey and mottled variations are on record, and this individual shows a partial change of plumage. Unlike many other birds, the female courts the male.*

5th

Saw 12 Lesser Whitethroats frequenting a hedge-row at edge of Hickling Broad. As they flitted out one after the other they very much resembled young Great Tits.

The Moorhens are very partial to the apples or pears if any fall from the trees against Lodge; I saw one this morning from the window standing on the branch eating a pear upon the tree. Have found several of late, which I thought was the work of Thrushes or Blackbirds, which no doubt was after all the work of these Moorhens.

6th

Saw 4 Sandwich Terns and 2 Common on Hickling Broad.

Flushed a Solitary or Great Snipe on Wet Spurlings. It allowed me to almost tread on it before rising, and then only flew a short distance before settling again, similar to a Jack Snipe. There were a good number of full Snipe on, which is a good place, and in the right condition for them.

OSPREY *A rare visitor to Hickling in the spring or autumn. One of the only three birds of prey that hover, the others being the kestrel and the rough-legged buzzard. To see an osprey hover over water, then suddenly close its wings and plunge downwards to make a strike at a fish, is an unforgettable sight; rarely does a strike fail. Its food consists solely of fish.*

7th

At 6 a.m. this morning saw an Osprey in Ball's Corner hovering over the water after fish. It came on to White Slea, and came so close to the Lodge that I thought it was going to alight on the large willow trees in front of Lodge. It came past me on Hickling and, after flying about a short time, went off toward the sea.

8th

Wind E. Very hot day. At 8 p.m. a gale sprung up from N., vivid flashes of lightning illuminated the sky. Heavy rain.

Was looking out of window this morning and saw a Common Sandpiper on the quay heading, and twice it went into my punt which was lying alongside.

Saw a Curlew Sandpiper close to where the duck are fed at Horsey.

9th

Was out early this morning and saw several waders going E., Knots, Dunlins, Ringed Plovers, Curlew, 2 Greenshanks, 7 Reeves.

Saw 6 Lesser Whitethroats, 3 Willow Wrens, and a young Pied Flycatcher against Lodge.

There are plenty of Meadow Pipits and a decided increase of Reed Buntings about to-day.

11th

Saw 2 Pied Flycatchers and some Willow Wrens.

⟞ 14th ⟝

Saw a Rough-legged Buzzard this morning
  preying on the marshes.

⟞ 15th ⟝

Very strong wind from N.W.
Saw 6 Pied Flycatchers and Whitethroats, also
  Willow Wrens seeking the sheltered places.

⟞ 16th ⟝

Saw an immature Black Tern on Hickling Broad.
Saw some young Swallows in the nest to-day, and
  young House Martins looking out of the nest.

CURLEW SANDPIPER *(left, top)* *A rare visitor to*
Hickling on its autumn migration. Named after the
similarity of its beak to that of the curlew. Flight is
strong, showing the distinctive white rump.

SANDWICH TERN *(left, bottom)* *The largest of the tern*
family, and named after the town of Sandwich, Kent,
where it was first observed in 1786. Large breeding
colonies are spread around all of Britain's coastline.
Flight is strong and rapid.

ROUGH-LEGGED BUZZARD *(right)* *A rare visitor to*
Norfolk in early spring or autumn. Distinguished from
the common buzzard by its feathered legs and white tail
with broad black band at the end; in flight it is bolder and
the white on the tail is prominent. Prefers open
marshland to wooded areas.

⇒ 19th ⇐

Saw on Heigham Sounds one of the most remarkable specimens of the Bearded Tit I've ever seen. It was with 6 or 7 others and was a uniform cream colour. Have never seen one like it before. No doubt it is a freak.

⇒ 20th ⇐

2 Slavonian Grebes on Hickling Broad.

⇒ 21st ⇐

Flushed 2 Corn Crakes and a Spotted Crake. A Corn Crake was brought to me by a man who thought it 'an uncommon bird'.

SLAVONIAN GREBE *(left) An infrequent autumn visitor to Norfolk. Also known as the 'horned grebe' because of the breeding male's golden ear-tufts, which are set higher than those of the black-necked grebe. Chiefly seen as a solitary bird.*

MERLIN *(right, mobbing a buzzard) A winter visitor, preying on small birds such as meadow pipits which it chases on the wing and catches with its long talons; will also chase larger birds, such as this buzzard, just for the love of it. Not as fast as the hobby or peregrine falcon.*

BUZZARD *Less common in Norfolk than in north and west of England and Scotland. Sluggish in its habits, though when on the wing it can be remarkably graceful.*

Saw a Common Buzzard this evening being mobbed by 1,000 Starlings. They looked like a swarm of bees, so much so that the Buzzard was scarcely visible.

22nd

Wind N.E. Squally, calm clear evening.

Saw the Common Buzzard on Deary's Marsh. It came very close to me, and is marked very much like a young Rough-legged. It looks about the size of a Marsh Harrier.

As I was writing indoors at dusk this evening with the window open, heard the Bittern call close to Lodge. I rushed out of doors and saw it overhead about 40 yards high. I tried to imitate its call by sounding at intervals awk, awk, awk, and it answered back, and circled overhead 6 times, making circles of 100 yards or so. This is the first time I've tried calling the Bittern, and if opportunity serves, will try it again to see if it is really possible to decoy by imitating its sound.

There are few sounds upon a calm evening on the Broad as charming as the sound of a Bittern.

LESSER GREY SHRIKE *Rare autumn visitor to Norfolk. Distinguishable from the great grey shrike by its broader black eyeband and length of primaries. Its food consists of beetles and other insects which it eats whilst holding them in its foot.*

——◁ 25th ▷——

Saw a Merlin tormenting the Common Buzzard
  this morning.

——◁ 26th ▷——

Near the White Slea Wood, where the furze
  bushes and small hawthorn bushes are dotted on
  the marsh, saw without doubt a Lesser Grey
  Shrike. I watched it for some time go from one
  bush to another, and saw it fly on to the ground
  after food which it ate on the bushes, quite six
  times. It came and perched on a bush after
  waiting an hour secreted amongst the furze
  about 30 yards away.
After looking it up in Howard Saunders
  [*Saunders' 'An Illustrated Manual of British
  Birds'*], should say it was an immature bird, as
  there was no trace of black forehead, but a
  uniform grey, and the black on tail and the wings
  was not so intense as would be upon an adult.
  Any rate it was not the Great Grey; it looked
  about the size of a Red-back [*Red-backed Shrike*],
  though I see it is about an inch longer.

CROSSBILL *Resident all year in conifer forests, and
from autumn to spring moves around in small flocks. Its
tough crossed bill, unique amongst British birds, is
adapted to pick the seeds out of conifer cones, its main
food. It will also eat insects and berries.*

27th

Saw 6 Crossbills at Gibbs Wood, could only see one adult or red one amongst them. They were feeding on the fir cones.

Saw 2 Long-eared Owls sitting amongst the branches of the young firs.

Heard the Bittern at dusk.

Lesser Grey Shrike is upon the same ground as yesterday, after watching it for some time have no doubt as to correct identity of such a rare visitor.

28th

Have noticed several small flocks of Siskins, Redpolls, Goldfinches going S.W. today.

Saw 4 Wheatears on the marshes and a Whinchat near Lodge.

29th

A Marsh Harrier (mature male). The wings and tail were a pearl grey equal to those of a male Montagu. It rose so close (15 yards), could see the yellow legs and feet, and the creamy head which was not so distinct as in the other Marsh Harriers I've seen. This is the first time I've ever seen such a mature male. It had been feeding upon a Moorhen.

30th

Terrible gale sprung up this morning from N.W. Heavy rain squalls.

Saw dozens of Common Terns that were blown about like straws.

Gulls by the hundreds came unto Hickling Broad, and amongst them saw 2 Richardson's Skuas.

The Starlings that usually roost in the reed beds were unable to secure a footing and flew hither and thither in huge flocks. They were blown into collision with each other and I actually saw one drop from a flock, no doubt with a damaged wing.

MARSH HARRIER *See page 94.*

OCTOBER

1st

Gale raging all day from N. with heavy rain squalls. High tide.

Was out early this morning hunting for a fisherman staying in the village who had not returned off the Broad all night. Could find no trace of him or his boat. Swell was rolling 4 feet high on Hickling, and found it the toughest punting in my life.

Thousands of Gulls were about, amongst them saw Iceland Gull, 3 Richardson's Skuas, 2 Shearwaters (probably Manx), 1 Little Gull (immature), 21 Sandwich Terns, plenty of Common or Arctic [*Terns*].

Must have seen 100 Snow Buntings going S.W. during the day, besides Redpolls, Siskins, and other finches.

ICELAND GULL *A rare visitor to Hickling on its autumn migration. When at rest the wing tips are not crossed, which makes the body look tapered. Maturity is not reached until the fourth year. It has a distinctive loud, shrill call.*

Saw 3 Hooded Crows, 10 Golden Plovers, plenty of full [*Common*] Snipe, 6 Jack Snipe, 1 Woodcock in Gibbs Wood.

Very few duck indeed seen.

3rd

Saw two Bramblings in company with some Chaffinches.

A flock of Geese (17) came over Lodge about 100 yards up, going W., probably Pink-footed, a flock of about 20 Widgeon kept wheeling around them, which caused them to break their line of formation.

4th

Saw 4 Common Terns playing about on Hickling Broad.

One Dabchick, 2 Slavonians, and a Red-throated Diver on Hickling too.

A Green Woodpecker came and fed for some time around the trees surrounding Lodge.

5th

Saw 4 Snow Buntings this morning.

Stonechats more in evidence.

6th

The Coots are in good numbers, too many on Sounds.

Counted 6 Kestrels hovering on the marshes at back of Lodge, where a Barn Owl seeks for food at sundown.

7th

Flushed the Bittern from edge of one of the roadways through reeds on Sounds. It rose about 3 feet from head of punt, but never made any noise.

8th

Saw a Dabchick in front of quay heading at Lodge, also Kingfisher which daily comes after the small fry.

9th

Saw a Merlin chasing a Greenfinch.

10th

Saw a Willow Wren and quite half a dozen Goldcrests in Town Wood, also Treecreepers, one Lesser Spotted Woodpecker, Blue, Marsh, Coal, Great and Long-tailed Tits.

Saw a flock of 30 Bramblings, and several family parties of Goldfinches.

11th

There are large flocks of Peewits on the marshes.

Saw a Goldeneye, 2 Widgeon and a Slavonian Grebe on Horsey Mere.

Gulls come regularly in thousands to Hickling and Horsey Broads for fresh water from the North Sea.

Bittern calling at dusk.

14th

Crows, Rooks, Jackdaws, Starlings, Larks, are migrating S.W. in good numbers.

Have seen to-day a good number of Redwings and Ring Ouzels, some of the latter being in very good plumage.

A good number of Snipe are about: the full are flying about in 'wisps'.

A few Pochard and Tufted Ducks have arrived.

GREENFINCH *(chased by a merlin) Sometimes called the 'green linnet', this sociable bird is common in localities well supplied with trees and bushes in large gardens. Its song is a rapid twitter, and in song flight the male circles round with slowly flapping wings. Usually raises two or even three broods in a season.*

MERLIN *See page 106.*

16th

Bearded Tits are distributed all over the ground where any reeds grow.
Saw a Little Grebe [*Dabchick*] on Sounds.

17th

There are a great number of Goldcrests over. Caught one inside the new room at Lodge, and Linkhorn caught one indoors at his house too. Saw a dozen in view at once around the trees and bushes.

COAL TIT *(top left) Differs from other black-capped and white-cheeked tits by large white patch on nape. A shy bird, with a plaintive song sweeter and clearer in tone than that of other British tits.*

GOLDCREST *(top right) Smallest British bird, not common at Hickling. It is fearless despite its size; a female will attack any bird which threatens its nest.*

STONECHAT *(bottom left) Fairly uncommon at Hickling. Prefers neglected terrain to cultivated areas, perching on top of bushes and gorse whilst flicking the wings and spreading the tail. Call note sounds like two stones being struck together.*

GOLDFINCH *(bottom right) Small flocks are known as 'charms'. In trees, it perches on outer twigs rather than amongst the foliage. Does not mix freely with other species. Feeds mainly on seed heads, flitting about them like a butterfly.*

Saw a Great Grey Shrike.
The Bittern was flying around White Slea at twilight, about 10 minutes earlier than other times, so Linkhorn who was with me saw it too for first time. As there was a breeze blowing it did not call once, and have noticed time and again how quietly they move about if any wind is blowing, while on the other hand they are noisy when it is a dead calm. They fly slower than Heron against wind.

20th

When sailing across Hickling Broad this afternoon, saw a Little Gull in company with a few Black-headed and Common Gulls flitting about just on top of water. I sailed the punt so it passed within 20 yards of me and saw it was an adult, as the pure white tail and the white on primaries and secondaries were visible.

21st

Seen 2 Great Grey Shrikes near Lodge, a Peregrine Falcon going E. about 40 yards high, and a female Hen-harrier mobbed by 2 Crows (Hoodies).
Flushed a Short-eared Owl to-day.

23rd

Blackbird (male) at Hickling with pure white tail, and about two primary feathers on each wing white.

24th

Saw a Little Gull (adult) on Hickling, whether it is the same bird as I saw on the 20th, cannot say.

Also saw on Hickling a Slavonian Grebe, 5 immature Goldeneyes.

The Coots are leaving the reeds now for the open Broad.

Saw the female Hen-harrier.

25th

Saw 29 Bewick's Swans in the afternoon, which settled in two companies in Ball's Corner, after having a short feed, and harassed by the Mutes they went off W. at dusk. They were all old birds.

BLACKBIRD *(left) Pied varieties and albinos are not uncommon, but this particular bird must have looked striking in flight. Has a powerful and beautiful song, and a noisy alarm note when disturbed.*

KESTREL *(right) The most abundant of British birds of prey. Flies with fast wing beats and occasional short glides, then hovers with head to wind, rapidly flapping wings and depressed and outspread tail, as it scans the ground below. It pounces on its prey from an average height of twenty to thirty feet.*

26th

Sharp frost this morning. Wind W. Rain.

Saw 4 Snow Buntings, Bramblings, Goldfinches, Mealy and Lesser Redpolls, Siskins, and a Hawfinch which is rare here.

Seen the Great Grey Shrike and the female Hen-harrier.

Saw a Slavonian Grebe upon White Slea, and another on Hickling Broad.

28th

Nudd and I saw a beautiful Snow Bunting near Pleasure Island. It is one of the best I've ever seen.

29th

There was such a commotion amongst the fowl on the upper portion of Sounds this morning, that I was obliged to go, thinking it was someone pike fishing, as this portion is not thrown open until February. When I arrived a flock of Pochard rose from the open water, and the Coots were driving about in solid masses, and there in front of me, where the Pochard had risen from, was an Otter with a male Pochard in its mouth. Its wings were extended in its dying struggles, the Otter taking it under a few yards, as if smothering his victims was part of his slaying methods.

The Pochard, Coots, etc. were very wary about settling down, it having scared them very much.

30th

Saw a Great Grey Shrike which I suddenly surprised. It was feeding upon a Hedge Sparrow amongst some furze near the Town Wood. It had only eaten the brains and could not have been killed very long as the Sparrow was warm; I sat down about 100 yards away and it returned in 15 minutes to it again.

Flushed two Short-eared Owls from a marsh.

31st

Saw a Long-eared Owl and Barn Owl sitting amongst the ivy on the same tree, about 4 feet apart.

There are good numbers of Siskins and Redpolls of both species [*Lesser and Mealy*] frequenting the alder trees, and Goldfinches are to be seen almost everywhere.

Saw the female Hen-harrier.

SNOW BUNTING *A winter visitor to Hickling, usually seen in flocks moving rapidly over the ground as they feed on grass seeds. The white wings are most noticeable during flight.*

NOVEMBER

➼ 1st ➻

Saw a House Martin flitting about under the leeside of trees at Hickling Staithe [*the public landing stage on the Broad*]. I saw one at the same place during a snowstorm, Nov. 15th 1904, which is a very late date.

Saw the Bittern at dusk when coming from Horsey, flying towards Heigham Sounds.

➼ 3rd ➻

The 4 Bewick's Swans have been on Hickling Broad. They are not very shy, allowing one to sail within 50 yards of them. I noticed that when within 100 yards of them, they start bobbing their heads up and down.

BEWICK'S SWAN *(left) A winter visitor, named after the artist and bird illustrator Thomas Bewick. Smaller than the whooper swan, with a shorter bill. When taking off, it jumps straight into the air, unlike the larger mute swan which has to run on the water to get airborne.*

YELLOWHAMMER *(right) Known locally as a 'yellow gooley'. Its song is traditionally transcribed as 'a little bit of bread and no cheese', with the last note higher pitched. A sociable bird, often found with other seed-eaters.*

123

4th

There are only two Bewicks to-day on Hickling. These have at intervals been over Potter Heigham and Hickling villages, and paid Horsey Mere a visit. Have never seen them more than 25 yards high yet, and besides have never known Bewicks to stay so long.

Seen two Merlins to-day, both of them had food.

5th

Gale raging from W. all day and night.

Thousands of Gulls are on Hickling Broad, and have been streaming by White Slea practically the whole day.

6th

Saw the Hen-harrier in the early morning come past Lodge.

There were three Snow Buntings frequenting the shores of Big Rande to-day.

3 Scaups, a few Tufted Ducks and about a dozen Pochard.

8th

Saw the female Hen-harrier come and perch on one of the stakes around the decoy in front of Lodge.

There are very few Pochard or ducks of any kind on the Broads. Have never known such a scarcity for this time of year, and cannot understand the cause.

11th

There are a good number of Short-eared Owls on the marshes.

Saw female Hen-harrier.

Kingfishers are more frequently seen now. Saw three at one time in front of Lodge.

13th

Saw a Shorelark at the edge of Big Rande which was very tame. It was running along on the washings (weeds and bits of rushes brought up by high water and stranded). Have only seen two others here some seven years ago. Have seen about 6 others on the seashore.

Saw 11 Bewick's Swans going W. about 100 yards up.

The Snipe (Common) are in good numbers upon the randes etc., as the water is rather low just now and in just the right condition for them.

SHORE LARK *A very rare visitor to Hickling. There is a record of five birds shot at Great Yarmouth in 1876. Shown here in breeding plumage, with its distinctive tufts of narrow black feathers forming 'horns' over each eye. It is a tame and confiding species.*

━━━ 14th ━━━

Saw about 30 Pochard on Horsey, also 10 Widgeon, 3 immature Goldeneyes, 4 Scaups, and 6 Tufted Ducks. 40 Teal in Brayden marshes, that were put up by the female Hen-harrier.

Saw 2 Grey Wagtails on the rande in front of Lodge, they were feeding at the water-edge, and it was interesting to watch their movements. They are very uncommon here.

━━━ 15th ━━━

Saw three adult Common Scoters upon Hickling Broad. These are the best I've ever seen. They allowed me to sail within 25 yards of them before taking to wing.

━━━ 16th ━━━

There are great quantities of Peewits about to-day. Some of the flocks containing 500 and 600.

Saw the Hen-harrier in Deary's Marsh, the Teal and Snipe cleared off in front of it.

Three Curlews came by the Lodge.

GADWALL *An uncommon visitor, mainly in the winter months, although East Anglia attracts the majority of those that breed in Britain. Prefers lakes and well-hidden slow streams, but can also be seen resting on estuaries and coasts during migration. The call note is a curious rattling croak.*

━━━ 17th ━━━

Saw an immature [*Great*] Northern Diver upon Hickling Broad. As it came flying down the Broad, thought at first sight it was a Goose coming. Heard of a big Diver being seen by one of the men two days previous, which no doubt is the one.

━━━ 18th ━━━

There are immense quantities of Gulls in from sea to-day. They reach from Hickling Broad to Horsey Mere without any perceptible break. The feathers from these hordes of Gulls at the end of the day after washing drift down to edge of reeds like a line of white foam. Sometimes a small party of them fly slowly over the Coots and so harass them that they form into a black mass. Have never seen a Gull attempt to take any except wounded ones.

Saw a Gadwall in Ball's Corner.

━━━ 21st ━━━

Strong cold wind from W. Sharp frost at night.

The Peewits have nearly all gone.

Snipe are scarcer to-day.

Saw an immense bunch of Teal come off Sounds going on to Hickling Broad. There were between 300 and 400. They were flying very low, and kept wheeling about.

23rd

Strong cold wind from E.

There are a few lots of strange Mallard and Pochards in to-day.

A Gadwall came and settled upon White Slea.

Lot of Tits especially Long-tails seeking the shelter of hedgerows and woods.

Flushed two Woodcocks in Town Wood. Heard of three others being seen. No doubt brought over by this wind.

Saw Great Grey Shrike.

25th

The Pochard have increased during the last two days, but they are yet in small numbers compared with other years. There were about 500 on Hickling and between 100 and 200 on Sounds.

Have seen lots of Siskins, Lesser and Mealy Redpolls, Goldfinches, Bullfinches, also hundreds of Yellow Buntings.

27th

Very thick foggy day.

Shot a Stoat just assuming its white winter coat.

Heard an adult Goldeneye upon Hickling, but never saw it.

LESSER REDPOLL *Less common at Hickling than in north and west of Britain. Darker and smaller than the mealy redpoll, also seen at Hickling. A tame and confiding species, and often seen in winter with other seed-eaters.*

28th

My father told me he saw one of the Great Grey Shrikes (probably male) have 30 or 40 trys to take a Meadow Pipit upon wing, and it was still attempting as far as he could see. The female no doubt was following about 40 yards high.

29th

There were quite 300 Pochard on Sounds to-day. This is the largest number thus far this year or season.

Coots have increased upon Hickling during the last few days. There are quite 1,500 now.

Several Treecreepers in the Woods.

30th

Saw 34 Geese (Pinkfoots). They came past Lodge going E. about 50 yards high. These Geese are often seen after a few days' foggy weather, no doubt from W. Norfolk, Holkham. They lose their bearings during foggy weather.

The adult Goldeneye with three immatures. The whistling or rattling sound of this bird's wings can be heard 600 to 700 yards away.

The female Hen-harrier has been working around Lodge.

TREECREEPER *Often unnoticed, owing to its small size, camouflaging colours and quick movements on trees. It hunts constantly for tree insects, climbing with feet wide apart, pressing its tail feathers against the bark like a woodpecker.*

DECEMBER

1st

There are a good number of Snipe about on the randes and marshes, owing to the water having fallen, which makes the ground ideal for them now.

Saw 2 Dabchicks in White Slea Dyke.

2nd

Saw a Great Grey Shrike in Horsey Brayden, also the Hen-harrier.

There are quite a lot of Jays in the Woods.

4th

There are about 400 to 500 Pochard come from the Sounds through Deep Dyke unto Hickling Broad at dusk.

Have never seen so many Barn Owls as of late, several of them are working about the marshes for food about 3 p.m. There are also several Short-eared Owls dotted over the marshes, and an occasional Long-eared may be seen before dusk.

TEAL *See page 49.*

5th

Wind strong from S. Heavy rain all morning, cleared in afternoon and sharp frost.

The Peewits were wheeling about the marshes they usually frequent in flocks of hundreds, which is generally a sign frost is near at hand, and sure enough it was upon us before dusk.

Redwings are as numerous as ever, but think that Fieldfares are much thinner in numbers compared with other years.

6th

Wind S.W. Raining all day.

Seen a male and female Merlin. Have never seen so many before as this autumn and winter.

Goldcrests are in great numbers especially amongst the furze bushes. The Common Wren is found all over the marshes, far from any habitation on bushes. I know of no bird more equally distributed over every kind of ground.

7th

Wind light from S.W. Rain in morning, cleared out and sharp frost.

There are several Snipe about, and Jacks seem to be fairly plentiful as one flushes them here and there, which is generally a sure sign they are commoner on their favourite grounds.

A few Teal keep upon Deary's Marsh, but they are very sensitive to frost.

11th

An immature Great Northern Diver passed over the village this morning about 20 yards high going towards the Broad, and was shot by a boy before reaching the Broad. Alfred Nudd saw it as it carried on and fell close by his house.

The Water Rails continue to feed around White Slea.

13th

Saw a Lesser Spotted Woodpecker and 2 Green Woodpeckers in the Town Wood.

There are a great number of Long-tailed Tits in the Woods, also a fair number of Marsh and Great Tits.

The Blue Tits are very partial to the reed beds.

WATER RAIL *(left)* *A most elusive bird, more often heard than seen ; its main call has been likened to the squealing of a pig. Breeds in marshy areas only.*

DABCHICK *(right)* *Also known as the 'little grebe'. The smallest of the grebes, and the only European one that never has a crest or ear-tufts. More inclined to fly than other grebes, but only for short distances.*

14th

Linkhorn tells me that owing to the restlessness of Pochard upon Sounds, he went towards upper portion, and just on the left of entrance he heard a crackling sound, and quietly moved forward, coming upon an Otter ('a great old warmin' as he described it) laying upon its side eating a fish. It quickly disappeared upon seeing him, and he also found the head, feet and wings of a Pochard.

There were about 300 Pochard upon Sounds, also two Bewick's Swans.

16th

Have seen a great number of Siskins and Lesser Redpolls to-day, principally upon the alders, also a good number of Goldfinches and Bullfinches.

Saw a Rough-legged Buzzard and Hooded Crow fighting upon the marshes.

Short-eared Owls came past at dusk.

17th

Saw a Lesser Woodpecker in the Town Wood.

GREAT TIT *Very pugnacious, and will attack small and weak birds, splitting their skulls with its powerful beak to get at their brains. Has a vast repertoire of calls that are difficult to analyse.*

Noticed Goldfinches, Siskins, Lesser Redpolls feeding in the alder trees.

19th

Flushed two Jack Snipe. The full Snipe are very small in numbers just now.

A few Herons frequent the marshes.

Coots are in good numbers, 1,500 to 2,000 should say.

20th

Calm in morning, gale sprung up from W. Raining hard all day.

Saw female Hen-harrier near Lodge.

There were quite 600 Pochard upon Horsey to-day, also 2 adult Goldeneyes in company with a dozen immatures, several Tufted Ducks, and a small Grebe, which judging by its size might be an Eared [*Black-necked*] Grebe.

There were hundreds of Peewits in the marshes, which I noticed some two hours before the gale went up to great height and appeared as mere specks, wheeling about into all fantastic shapes.

WREN *Also known as the 'jenny wren', because of its diminutive size. It is constantly on the move, hunting for insects, and only occasionally does it come into the open. It makes a slight ticking noise during all its movements.*

22nd

Saw the Eared Grebe which took to wing and flew
to the other end of the Mere.
Snipe are very thin. Several Jack still linger with
us.

25th

Wind W. Heavy rain evening.

26th

Saw a Great Grey Shrike take a Blue Tit from a
bush and fly away 100 yards with it in its claws.

GOOSANDER *(left, two females) The largest of Britain's
saw-billed ducks, and a winter visitor to Hickling. Flies
close to the water, following the bend of a river. The male
has a dark-green head and grey rump, with pink
underparts.*

GREAT GREY SHRIKE *(right, carrying a blue tit) A
regular winter visitor, more partial to wooded country
than other shrikes. Also known as the 'butcher bird'
because of its habit of impaling its victims on long, sharp
thorns prior to eating them.*

➤27th ➤

Saw 2 female Goosanders upon Hickling Broad. Watched them fishing some 200 yards away. They move at a great speed, going 50 to 60 yards between every dive.

➤28th ➤

Saw 5 Water Rails and 3 Moorhens feeding around back of Lodge. They appeared to be very sociable.

Seen several flocks of Wood-pigeons migrating S.W.

Saw a flock of 8 Teal on Deary's Marsh. These birds are very scarce with us during January and February.

➤29th ➤

Owing to the mild weather the Coots upon Hickling are very noisy as if pairing off. They take more readily to reeds when like this.

Mistle and Song Thrushes are singing away in the Woods at morning and evening.

MISTLE THRUSH *Largest resident thrush breeding all over Britain, named after its love of mistletoe berries. A quarrelsome bird, especially in the nesting period. The larger size, greyer upper parts and more boldly spotted underparts distinguish it from the song thrush.*

➤30th ➤

Light breeze from W. Warm day.

Heard a Snipe drum at twilight and saw the bird on its downward flight. It only did it once. This is the earliest I've ever heard it, and was surprised to hear it.

Saw the male Hen-harrier to-day. It looks to be a second-year bird. The female keeps about yet.

Fieldfares are more numerous just now than any time this season.

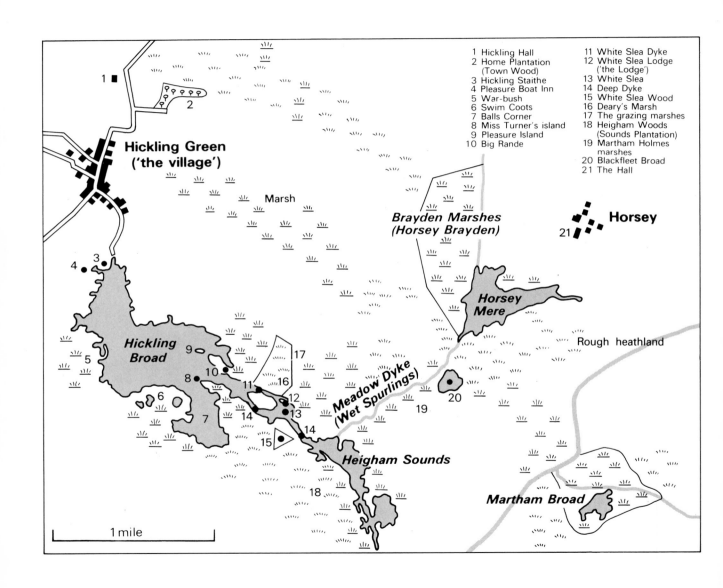

1 Hickling Hall
2 Home Plantation (Town Wood)
3 Hickling Staithe
4 Pleasure Boat Inn
5 War-bush
6 Swim Coots
7 Balls Corner
8 Miss Turner's island
9 Pleasure Island
10 Big Rande
11 White Slea Dyke
12 White Slea Lodge ('the Lodge')
13 White Slea
14 Deep Dyke
15 White Slea Wood
16 Deary's Marsh
17 The grazing marshes
18 Heigham Woods (Sounds Plantation)
19 Martham Holmes marshes
20 Blackfleet Broad
21 The Hall

Hickling Green ('the village')

Marsh

Brayden Marshes (Horsey Brayden)

21 Horsey

Horsey Mere

Rough heathland

Hickling Broad

Meadow Dyke (Wet Spurlings)

Heigham Sounds

Martham Broad

1 mile

Complete summary
of bird sightings

This list includes all details about the quantity, gender and age of the birds noted in the original diary; gender is indicated here by the abbreviations (m.) and (f.). In the absence of a more specific indication of the numbers seen, the name of a species is given in the singular or plural, as in the diary. In the case of species whose names do not take a plural ending (such as snipe, mallard, scaup), and where there are no additional details of age or gender to make it clear whether more than one bird is meant, the name is followed where necessary by the abbreviation (p.) to indicate a plural.

January

1st   Goldeneye (adult m.)
2nd   Coots (2), Pheasant, Richard's Pipit
3rd   Hen-harrier (f.), Goldeneye (adult m. with immatures), Bearded Tits, Pochards, Tufted Ducks, Shovelers, Mallard (p.), Coots
4th   Coot, Pochard, Mallard, Bearded Tits
5th   Pochards, Tufted Duck, Black-throated Diver (immature)
6th   Goldeneye (adult), Hen-harrier (f.)
7th   Pochards (flock of 300), Goldeneye (20 immatures, 1 adult), Coots (35)
8th   *no diary entry*
9th   Snow Bunting, Wood-pigeons (flocks), Pochards (500)
10th   Great Grey Shrike, Merlin, Skylark, Goldeneye (adult with 30 immatures)
11th   Pochards, Hen-harrier (f.), Water Rails (5)
12th   Mallard (p.), Pochards (100+), Black-throated Diver, Goldeneye (2 adult m.)

13th   Geese, possibly Bean (10), Goldeneye (adult), Waxwing
14th   Shelducks (8 m., 6 f.), Coots
15th   *no diary entry*
16th   Coots (2,000), Grey Wagtail, Waxwing
17th   Coots, Pochards, Wood-pigeons (12), Hawfinches (2), Green Woodpeckers (3)
18th   Coots (2,000), Common Scoter, Goldeneye (2 adults, 30 immatures), Pochards (400–500)
19th   Pochards (100), Goosanders (1 m., 1 f.), Tufted Ducks (12), Smew (f. or immature m.)
20th   Smews (2 ?immatures), Rough-legged Buzzard, Rooks, Crows
21st   Mallard (p.), Pochards (100+)
22nd   Geese, possibly White-fronted (3)
23rd   Pochards (100s)
24th   Teal (6), Tufted Ducks (flock of 20), Scaup (m.), Goldeneye (2 adult m. with 30 immatures), Snow Bunting, Lapwings, Golden Plovers (6)
25th   Bullfinches, Great Spotted Woodpecker, Snipe (p.), Bearded Tits (flock of 10), Hen-harrier (f.)
26th   Coots (2,000), Pochards (500 to 600), Tufted Ducks, Goldeneye (p.), Mallard (p.)
27th   Mistle Thrushes, Green Woodpeckers (pair), Kestrels (pair), Wood-pigeons (26+)
28th   Pochards, Coots, Goldeneye (2 adults with 30 immatures)
29th   Green Woodpecker, Goldeneye (p.), Smew
30th   Pochards, Gadwall, Snipe (p.), Coots, Goldeneye (adults with immatures)
31st   Widgeon (12), Shovelers (7), Smew, Lapwings (flocks), Redwings, Larks, Fieldfares, Snipe (p.)

February

1st   Pochards, Coots
2nd   Coots (100), Pochards (100), Smews (3 ?immatures), Lapwings
3rd   Mallard (35), Great Grey Shrike, Stonechat (dead f.)

141

4th Hen-harrier (f.), Merlins (? 3)
5th *no diary entry*
6th Goldeneye (40 immatures with 1 adult m.), Great Crested Grebes (3)
7th Pochards, Teal (5), Snipe (p.), Shovelers (2), Black-headed Gulls (1,000)
8th Great Spotted Woodpeckers (2), Water Rails, Goldeneye (1 adult m. with immatures)
9th Mallard (19), Pochards, Tufted Ducks, Coots (2,000), Hen-harrier (f.)
10th Teal (4), Widgeon (5), Pochards (500), Woodcock, Short-eared Owls (2), Tufted Ducks, Dabchicks (2)
11th Black-headed Gulls (1,000), Herring Gulls, Pochards, Coots, Great Spotted.Woodpecker
12th *no diary entry*
13th Coots, Goldeneye (adult m. with 30 immatures)
14th Kestrels (pair), Goldcrests, Smews (4)
15th Pochards (450), Coots, Duck's nest (decoy) with 16 eggs
16th Great Grey Shrike, Lapwings, Green Woodpeckers (2), Great Spotted Woodpecker
17th Coots (14 shot), Mallard (11 shot), Jack Snipe (7 shot), Pigeon (shot), Pintails (pair), Teal (p.), Shovelers (12), Widgeon (2), Smews (5), Goldeneye (p.), Tufted Ducks
18th Coots (167 shot), Mallard (3 shot), Pochards (2 shot), Lapwing (shot)
19th *no diary entry*
20th Snipe, Redshanks (3)
21st-27th *no diary entry*
28th Mallard (p.), Teal (p.), Pochards, Goldeneye (2 adults with immatures), Snipe (p.), Lapwings, Redshanks

March

1st Great Crested Grebes (2 pairs), Goldeneye (4 adult m. with 20 immatures), Shovelers (8 f., 12 m.), Redshanks (4)
2nd Lapwings (flocks), Black-headed Gulls, Lesser Spotted Woodpeckers (2), Redwings, Fieldfares (35)

3rd Bearded Tits, Common Buzzard, Sparrowhawk
4th Mallard (p.), Widgeon (20), Pintails (2 m., 1 f.)
5th Great Crested Grebes (3), Tufted Ducks (7), Scaup (2), Pochards (15), Redshanks (10)
6th Teal (7), Goldeneye (3 adult), Widgeon (4 m., 6 f.), Pochards (30), Tufted Ducks (20), Redshanks (20), Snipe (p.), Jack Snipe (p.)
7th Redshanks, Lapwings, Hooded Crows, Rooks, Stock Doves
8th Shovelers (2 pairs), Coots (1,800), Hen-harrier (m.)
9th Hawfinch (shot, ? f.)
10th–18th *no diary entry*
19th Ringed Plovers (2), Redshanks
20th Goldeneye (4 immatures), Pochards (20), Tufted Ducks (13), Shovelers (pair), Great Crested Grebes (2 pairs)
21st Garganey (1 m., 2 f.), Blackbirds (100)
22nd Bearded Tits, Snipe's nest with 3 eggs
23rd Short-tailed Tits, Marsh Tits, Firecrests (2), Goldcrests
24th Fieldfares, Redwings, Hooded Crows, Barn Owl
25th Pintails (pair), Scaup (3), Tufted Ducks (7)
26th Teal (3 pairs), Shovelers (pair)
27th Great Tits, Dabchicks (pair)
28th Hen-harrier (f.), Moorhens, Water Rails
29th Great Crested Grebes (5), Pochards (13), Tufted Ducks (3), Scaup (m.), White-eyed Pochard (f.)
30th Shags (pair or 2 birds), Great Crested Grebes
31st Garganey (pair), Coot's nest with 2 eggs, Bearded Tits

April

1st Reeve, Redshanks, Garganey (3), Siskins (flock of 14), White-eyed Pochard (f.)
2nd *no diary entry*
3rd Lapwings, Snipe (p.), Golden Plovers (flock of 6)
4th Reeve, Widgeon (2 m., 4 f.), Teal (12), Goldeneye (immature), Long-eared Owl
5th Bramblings, Chaffinches, Long-tailed Tits, Treecreepers, Great Tits (6), Blue Tits (4)

6th Mallard, Teal (30), Shovelers (3 pairs), Garganey (7), Tufted Ducks (6), Pochards (20)

7th Garganey (f.), Reeve, Curlew, Woodcock, Jack Snipe (p.)

8th *no diary entry*

9th Mallard, Shoveler, Teal (4), Garganey (7), Pochard, White-eyed Pochard, Tufted Duck, Goldeneye, Widgeon, Great Crested Grebe, Coot, Snipe, Redshank, Reeve, Ringed Plover, Curlew, Golden Plover, Lapwing, Water Rail, Lesser Black-backed Gull, Herring Gull, Common Gull, Black-headed Gull, Heron, Kestrel, Carrion Crow, Hooded Crow, Rook, Jackdaw, Jay, Wood-pigeon, Stock Dove, Starling, Blackbird, Thrush, Redwing, Meadow Pipit, Moorhen, Robin, Stonechat, Skylark, Hedge Sparrow, Reed Bunting, Corn Bunting, Blue Tit, Coal Tit, Marsh Tit, Bearded Tit, Greenfinch, Sparrow, Pied Wagtail, Wren, ? Greater Black-backed Gull, ? Yellow Wagtail, Mute Swan's nest with 6 eggs

10th Dunlin (flocks), Ringed Plovers (flocks), Treecreepers, Marsh Tits, Robin's nest with 1 egg

11th Coots' nests (2 with 7 and 3 eggs), Teal (7 pairs), Garganey (2), Grey Plovers (4), Widgeon (17)

12th Lapwings' nests (4 with 1 egg in each), Redshank's egg, Common Tern

13th Bearded Tit's nest with 2 eggs, Garganey (2 pairs), White-eyed Pochard

14th Willow Warbler, White Wagtail, Moorhen's nest with 2 eggs, Mallard (14 young), Marsh Harrier (? f.)

15th Swallow, Bearded Tit's nest with 4 eggs, Coots' nests (3 with eggs), Reeve, Pochards (2), Widgeon (pair), Yellowhammers, Greenfinch

16th *no diary entry*

17th House Martins, Sand Martins, Willow Warblers, Common Sandpiper

18th Shelducks (pair), White-eyed Pochard, Tufted Duck (m.), Pochards (4)

19th Chaffinch's nest with 2 eggs, Blue Tits (pair)

Cuckoo

20th Black Tern, Reeves (3), Yellow Wagtails (pair), Cuckoo

21st Sedge Warblers, Whitethroats, Reeves (2), Lapwings (9), Garganey (pair)

22nd Garganey (pair), Shovelers (pair), Teal (2 pairs + 12), Bearded Tits' nests (2 with 5 eggs each), Widgeon (pair)

23rd Thrush's nest with 4 eggs, Cuckoo

24th Reeves (2), Green Sandpiper, Grasshopper Warbler, Snipe's nest with 4 eggs, Rough-legged Buzzard

25th Kestrel's nest with 4 eggs, Bearded Tit's nest, Bearded Tits (5 young), Nuthatch

26th Redshank's nest with 3 eggs, Reeves (4), Blue Tits, Bearded Tit's nest with hatching young, Jack Snipe (2)

27th Redshanks' nests (2 with 4 eggs in each), Meadow Pipit's nest with 1 egg, Garganey (pair), Teal (3 pairs), Shovelers (pair), Heron

28th Marsh Harrier (? m.)

29th Redstart (adult m.), Wheatear (m.), Fieldfares (2), Bramblings
30th ? Black-necked Grebes (2)

May

1st Spoonbill, Marsh Harrier
2nd Teal (2 pairs), Garganey (pair), Pochards (3 m.)
3rd Lesser Whitethroat, Grasshopper Warblers, Reeve, Water Rail with 9 eggs, Bearded Tit's eggs (5)
4th Ringed Plovers (3), Cuckoo's egg, Redshanks' nests (3 with 2 eggs in each), Snipe's nest with 3 eggs
5th Great Crested Grebe's nest with 3 eggs, Yellow Wagtail's nest, Black Tern, Black-necked Grebe, Blue Tit's nest with 3 eggs, Snipe's nest with 4 eggs
6th White-eyed Pochard, Tufted Ducks (2 m.), Pochards 2 m.), Great Crested Grebes
7th Reeve, Shoveler (m.), Spotted Redshank, Marsh Harrier, Great Crested Grebe's nest with 3 eggs, Bearded Tits' nests (inc. 2 with young)
8th Montagu's Harrier (immature m.), Grey Plovers (2), Knot (4)
9th Montagu's Harriers (pair)
10th Bearded Tits' nests (3 with 6 eggs and young), Whitethroats, Willow Warblers, Pintail (m.)
11th Nightingale, Garden Warblers, Pintail
12th Bearded Tits' nests (4: 2 with 7 and 6 eggs, 2 with young), Greenshank, Montagu's Harriers (pair)
13th Black-tailed Godwit, Swifts, Reed Warblers, Sedge Warbler's nest with 2 eggs
14th White-winged Black Terns (2), Black Terns (8)
15th Black Terns (4), Common Terns (3), Tufted Duck (m.), Garganey (m.), Sparrowhawk, Short-eared Owl
16th Pied Flycatcher (f.), Black Terns (2), Montagu's Harriers (pair)
17th Mallard (9 young)
18th Whimbrels (5), Common Tern, Willow Warbler's nest with 5 eggs

19th Bearded Tit's nest with hatching young, Skylarks (young), Montagu's Harrier (m.)
20th Montagu's Harriers (pair), Spotted Flycatchers (pair)
21st *no diary entry*
22nd Montagu's Harriers (pair), Common Sandpipers (2), Sedge Warbler's nest with 6 eggs, Grasshopper Warbler's nest with 5 eggs
23rd Montagu's Harriers (pair), Lesser Tern
24th Whimbrel, Redshanks (30), Grasshopper Warblers (young)
25th Great Crested Grebes (3 young), Great Crested Grebe's nest with 1 egg, Ringed Plovers (2), Montagu's Harrier (f.)
26th Montagu's Harriers (pair), Goldfinch's nest with young
27th Spoonbill, Knot, Redshanks
28th Garganey (f. with 8 young)
29th Knot, Greenshank, Sparrowhawk
30th Montagu's Harrier (f.), Reeve
31st Cormorant, Black Terns (3)

June

1st Montagu's Harrier's nest with one egg
2nd Montagu's Harriers (f., 3 pairs), Marsh Harrier, Coot, Pochard (f.)
3rd Common Tern, Montagu's Harrier's nest with 2 eggs, Montagu's Harriers (pair), Grasshopper Warbler's nest with young, Ruff, Shoveler (f.), Garganey (m.), Redshank, Snipe, Bearded Tit
4th Mallard, Knot, Ringed Plover, Ruff, Montagu's Harrier's nest, Montagu's Harriers (pair), Marsh Harrier
5th Teal, Ringed Plover, Dunlin, Montagu's Harriers' nests (3: 2 with 3 eggs each, 1 with 1 egg)
6th Kestrels (adult with young)
7th *no diary entry*
8th Montagu's Harriers' nests (3: 2 with 4 eggs each, 1 with 2 eggs), Montagu's Harrier (m.), Pheasant

144

9th   Snipe's nest with 2 eggs
10th Garganey (2 with young), Heron
11th Montagu's Harrier's nest with 2 eggs
12th Redshank
13th Black Tern, Geese, possibly Egyptian (9)
14th Lesser Terns (8), Common Terns (2), Black Terns (2), Grey Phalarope, Montagu's Harrier (f.)
15th Montagu's Harriers' nests (2 with eggs)
16th Lapwing, Pied Wagtail
17th Black Tern, Shag
18th *no diary entry*
19th Cuckoo, Yellow Wagtails (2), Shoveler (m.)
20th Curlews (2), Green Sandpiper
21st Heron, Great Crested Grebes (2 pairs with young), Shag, Redshanks
22nd Swift
23rd Montagu's Harriers (2 pairs), Reed Warbler's nest, Curlews
24th Mallard (p.)
25th Sparrowhawk, Curlews, Montagu's Harriers (2 pairs), Common Sandpiper

26th Reed Warblers' nests (2, 1 with 5 eggs), Montagu's Harriers (2 pairs), Lesser Redpoll
27th Montagu's Harriers (2 pairs), Yellow Wagtail's nest with 5 eggs, Green Sandpiper
28th Jays, Black Tern
29th *no diary entry*
30th Reeve, Starlings (3,000)

July

1st   Tufted Duck, Shovelers (6)
2nd   *no diary entry*
3rd   Bearded Tit's nest with 5 eggs, Gadwall
4th   Montagu's Harrier's nest with 1 young, Curlews, Shovelers (10), Garganey (9)
5th   Great Crested Grebes, Shovelers (5), Corn Bunting's nest
6th   Green Sandpiper, Common Scoter, Montagu's Harriers (2 young and 1 hatching)
7th   Pochards (2), Bitterns (f. with 1 young)
8th   Spotted Redshank, Bittern (young)
9th   *no diary entry*
10th Sparrowhawks (2)
11th Montagu's Harrier, Skylark, Tufted Ducks (6)
12th Corn Buntings, Nightjar's nest with 1 egg, Dunlin (3)
13th Montagu's Harriers, Yellow Wagtail
14th Whimbrel, Greenshank, Mallard, Shoveler, Teal, Yellow Wagtail's nest with eggs, Yellow Wagtail
15th Great Crested Grebes, Pied Wagtails, Yellow Wagtails
16th *no diary entry*
17th Garganey (11), Red-legged Partridge
18th Garganey (11), Teal (15)
19th Corn Bunting's nest with 4 eggs, Sand Martins
20th Tufted Ducks (2), Grasshopper Warbler's nest with 2 eggs, Garganey
21st Snipe
22nd Green Sandpipers (2), Ringed Plover, Mallard (p.)
23rd Redshanks, Greenshank

Garganey

145

24th Pintail, Yellowhammer's nest with 2 eggs
25th Black Terns (1 adult, 1 immature), Green Sandpiper, Tufted Ducks (2)
26th Snipe (p.), Black Tern, Montagu's Harrier (m.)
27th Wood Sandpiper, Snipe (p.), Reeves
28th Black Tern (young)
29th Tufted Ducks (immatures), Coots
30th Wood Sandpipers (5), Reeve, Tufted Ducks (3)
31st Bearded Tits (2), Sedge Warblers (2), Reed Warbler, Blue Tit, Pied Wagtail, House Sparrow

August

1st Mallard (p.), Shovelers, Tufted Ducks, Garganey (p.), Teal (p.), Spotted Redshanks (2), Wood Sandpipers, Little Stint, Common Sandpiper, Dunlin, Bearded Tits
2nd Garganey (p.), Dunlins, Curlews, Whimbrels, Common Sandpipers (12), Long-eared Owl
3rd Curlews (6), Green Sandpiper, Common Sandpipers (8), Nightjars (pair)
4th Black Tern (immature)
5th Common Terns (96), Reed Bunting's nest with 3 young, Grasshopper Warbler's nest with 3 eggs
6th *no diary entry*
7th Black Terns (adult, 2 immatures)
8th Common Terns (5), Ruff (immature), Reeves (3), Dunlin, Greenshank, Montagu's Harrier (m.)
9th Green Sandpipers (2), Black Terns (2 immatures)
10th Black-headed Gulls (immatures), Moorhens (young)
11th Common Terns (6), Green Sandpipers (4), Montagu's Harriers (f. and 3 young)
12th Greenshank, Curlews (8)
13th *no diary entry*
14th Marsh Harrier, Curlews (8)
15th Pochards (3), Little Stint, Common Sandpiper
16th Montagu's Harriers (3 young), Shovelers (2), Redshanks (3)
17th Marsh Harrier, Sand Martins (1000s), Swallows (1000s)

18th Reeve, Curlews (8), Lesser Whitethroats, Willow Warblers (2), Reed Warblers, Sedge Warblers, Teal (30), Mallard (p.)
19th Reed Warbler, Bittern, Marsh Harrier
20th Montagu's Harriers (f. with 3 young), Partridge
21st Pheasant (f., on nest), Jays (10), Sparrowhawks, Kestrel, Willow Warblers, Whitethroats, Reed Warblers
22nd Yellow Wagtails, Cuckoos, Curlews
23rd Marsh Harrier, Bar-tailed Godwits (5), Dunlin (p.), Ringed Plovers
24th Kingfisher, Swallows
25th Redshanks (7), Herons, Sand Martins (1000s), House Martins, Swallows
26th Ruff, Reeves (4), Gadwall, Shovelers (2)
27th Montagu's Harrier (f.), Pochards (12), Bearded Tits (young)
28th Black Terns (2 immatures), Spotted Crake, Land Rails (2), Bittern
29th Teal (40), Great Crested Grebes (young), Pochards (6)
30th Reeve, Dunlin (5), Greenshank, Ringed Plovers (2), Shoveler, Teal (12), Common Terns (5)
31st Avocets (3)

September

1st Partridges (100), Curlew Sandpipers (10), Grey Plovers (20), Bittern
2nd Goldfinch's nest with young, Tufted Ducks (3), Pochards (12) Montagu's Harriers (f. with 3 young)
3rd *no diary entry*
4th Reeves (6), Knot (p.), Grey Plovers, Robin
5th Lesser Whitethroats (12), Pochards (4), Moorhen
6th Sandwich Terns (4), Common Terns (2), Great Snipe, Snipe (p.)
7th Osprey
8th Common Sandpiper, Curlews, Curlew Sandpiper, Bearded Tit (young)

9th Knot (p.), Dunlin (p.), Ringed Plovers, Curlew, Greenshanks (2), Reeves (7), Lesser Whitethroats (6), Willow Warblers (3), Pied Flycatcher (young), Meadow Pipits, Reed Buntings, Swift, Swallows, Sand Martins

10th *no diary entry*

11th Pied Flycatchers (2), Lapwings, Larks, Willow Warblers

12th Pochards (16), Tufted Ducks (3), Dabchick, Bittern, Larks

13th Greenshanks (4), Bar-tailed Godwits (10), Common Terns (4)

14th Rough-legged Buzzard, Widgeon (10), Tufted Ducks (3), Pochards (30), Lapwings

15th Common Terns (4), Dunlin (flocks), Pied Flycatchers (3), Whitethroats (3)

16th Black Tern (immature), Jack Snipe, Dunlin (40), Pied Flycatchers (2), Redstart (young), Swallows (young), House Martins (young)

17th Lapwings (flocks), Bittern

18th Pied Flycatchers (2), Willow Warbler, Widgeon (11), Pochards (30), Larks

19th Bearded Tits (7), Widgeon (2), Pochards (3)

20th Pochards (10), Tufted Ducks (5), Shoveler (m.), Slavonian Grebes (2)

21st Jack Snipe (4), Common Snipe (p.), Teal (30), Corncrakes (3), Spotted Crake, Common Buzzard, Starlings (1000s)

22nd Meadow Pipits, White Wagtails, Common Buzzard, Bittern

23rd Gulls, Lapwings, Skylarks, Redwings (2), Willow Warbler, Cuckoos (2 young)

24th *no diary entry*

25th Merlin, Great Crested Grebes (22), Goldcrests (2)

26th Lesser Grey Shrike

27th Crossbills (6), Long-eared Owls (2), Bittern, Lesser Grey Shrike

28th Widgeon (6), Gadwall (2), Pochards (15), Tufted Ducks (4), Siskins (flock), Redpolls (flock), Goldfinches (flock), Larks, Lapwings, Wheatears (4), Whinchat

29th Red-throated Diver (immature), Marsh Harrier (m.), Swift, Swallows, Sand Martins, House Martins

30th Common Terns, Gulls, Richardson's Skuas (2), Starlings (1000s)

October

1st Gulls (1000s), Iceland Gull, Richardson's Skuas (3), ? Manx Shearwaters (2), Little Gull (immature), Sandwich Terns (21), Snow Buntings (100), Redpolls, Siskins, various Finches, Hooded Crows (3), Golden Plovers (10), Snipe (p.), Woodcock

2nd Various Finches, Larks, Starlings, Crows, Lapwings, Cuckoo (young)

3rd Land Rail, Bramblings (2), Chaffinches, ? Pink-footed Geese (17), Widgeon (20)

4th Common Terns (4), Dabchick, Slavonian Grebes (2), Red-throated Diver, Green Woodpecker

5th Snow Buntings (4), Stonechats, Rough-legged Buzzard

6th Pochards, Tufted Ducks, Widgeon (p.), Teal (p.), Coots, Kestrels (6)

Common gull

7th Bittern, Widgeon (30), Mallard (p.)
8th Lapwings, Dabchick, Kingfisher
9th Hooded Crows, Larks, Starlings, Merlin, Greenfinch, Common Tern
10th Willow Warbler, Goldcrests (6), Treecreepers, Lesser Spotted Woodpecker, Blue Tits, Marsh Tits, Coal Tits, Great Tits, Long-tailed Tits, Bramblings (30), Goldfinches
11th Lapwings, Goldeneye, Widgeon (2), Slavonian Grebe, Gulls (1000s), Bittern
12th Hooded Crows, Larks, Starlings, Pochards (60), Tufted Ducks (60), Kingfisher, Teal (54)
13th Hooded Crows, Slavonian Grebe, Widgeon (2), Pochards (2)
14th Crows, Rooks, Jackdaws, Starlings, Larks, Redwings, Ring Ouzels, Lapwings, Snipe (p.), Tufted Ducks, Pochards
15th *no diary entry*
16th Pochards, Tufted Ducks, Goldeneye (3 immatures), Widgeon (p.), Mallard (p.), Bearded Tits, Dabchick,

Pintail

Lapwings, Crows, Rooks, Jackdaws, Redwings, Starlings
17th Goldcrests, Great Grey Shrike, Bittern, Pochards
18th Kingfishers (2), Dabchick, Pochard, Tufted Duck, Scaup (3), Goldeneye (2 immatures), Goldfinches (flocks)
19th Crows, Rooks, Jackdaws, Starlings, Larks, Redwings, Lapwings, Green Woodpecker, Sparrowhawks, Rock Pipits (2)
20th Little Gull, Black-headed Gulls, Common Gulls, Ring Ouzels, Redwings, Fieldfares
21st Pochards, Tufted Ducks, Crows, Jackdaws, Great Grey Shrikes (2), Peregrine, Hen-harrier (f.), Hooded Crows (2), Short-eared Owl
22nd *no diary entry*
23rd Widgeon (30), Pintails (2), Blackbird (m.), Crows, Rooks, Jackdaws
24th Little Gull, Slavonian Grebe, Goldeneye (5 immatures), Coots, Hen-harrier (f.), Green Woodpeckers, Great Spotted Woodpecker
25th Scaup (10), Pochards (100), Tufted Ducks (25), Gulls (1000s), Bewick's Swans (29), Mute Swans
26th Snow Buntings (4), Bramblings, Goldfinches, Mealy Redpolls, Lesser Redpolls, Siskins, Hawfinch, Great Grey Shrike, Hen-harrier (f.), Slavonian Grebes (2)
27th Merlin, Hen-harrier (f.), Rough-legged Buzzard, Golden Plovers (50), Kingfishers
28th Snow Buntings, Crows, Rooks, Jackdaws, Larks, Finches, Pochards (150), Tufted Ducks, Scaup (30)
29th Pochards (flock), Coots
30th Pochards, Great Grey Shrike, Short-eared Owls (2)
31st Woodcock, Long-eared Owl, Barn Owl, Siskins, Redpolls, Goldfinches, Hen-Harrier (f.)

November

1st House Martin, Jays, Sparrowhawks, Green Woodpeckers, Bittern

2nd Bewick's Swans (4), Pintail, Shoveler, Goldeneye (8 immatures), Scaup (p.), Tufted Ducks, Pochards, Rooks, Starlings, Pied Wagtails

3rd Bewick's Swans (4), House Martin, Wood-pigeons (200), Woodcock

4th Bewick's Swans (2), Merlins (2), Woodcock (2), Snipe (p.)

5th Gulls (1000s), Pochards, Tufted Ducks

6th Hen-harrier, Snow Buntings (3), Goldeneye (8 immatures), Scaup (3), Tufted Ducks, Pochards (12)

7th Snipe (p.), Teal (50–80), Short-eared Owls (2)

8th Hen-harrier (f.), Pochards

9th Bewick's Swans (7), Pochards, Rooks (1000s), Starlings (1000s), Crows (1000s), Pigeons (1000s), Tits, Long-tailed Tits, Bittern

10th Gulls (1000s), Jackdaws (1000s), Starlings (1000s), Larks (1000s), Fieldfares (1000s), Redwings (1000s), Bewick's Swans (2), Pink-footed Geese (13), Black-throated Diver (adult)

11th Wood-pigeons (flocks), Short-eared Owls, Hen-harrier (f.), Kingfishers (3)

12th *no diary entry*

13th Bewick's Swans (11), Shore Lark, Snipe (p.)

14th Woodcock, Pochards (30), Widgeon (10), Goldeneye (3 immatures), Scaup (4), Tufted Ducks (6), Teal (40), Hen-harrier (f.), Grey Wagtails (2)

15th Common Scoters (3), Pochards (200), Wood-pigeons

16th Lapwings, Hen-harrier, Teal, Snipe, Curlews (3), Fieldfares

17th Scoters, Great Northern Diver (immature), Merlins (2), Golden Plovers (150)

18th Gulls (1000s), Gadwall

19th *no diary entry*

20th Snipe (p.), Golden Plovers, Great Northern Diver, Pochards (300), Teal (100), Mallard (p.)

21st Lapwings, Snipe (p.), Teal (300–400)

22nd Water Rails (4), Golden Plovers

23rd Mallard (p.), Pochards, Gadwall, Tits, Long-tailed Tits, Woodcock (2), Great Grey Shrike

24th Mallard (500), Bramblings (flocks), Long-tailed Tits

25th Mallard (p.), Pochards (600), Widgeon (p.), Pintails (3), Gadwall (2), Siskins, Lesser Redpolls, Mealy Redpolls, Goldfinches, Bullfinches, Yellowhammers

26th *no diary entry*

27th Goldeneye

28th Great Grey Shrike, Goldeneye (adult with 3 immatures), Pochards, Mallard (p.)

29th Pochards (300), Coots (1,500), Treecreepers, Golden Plovers (flocks)

30th Pink-footed Geese (34), Pochards (500), Goldeneye (adult with 3 immatures), Hen-harrier

December

1st Goldeneye (6 immatures), Snipe (p.), Dabchicks (2)

2nd Great Grey Shrike, Hen-harrier, Pochards (400), Tufted Ducks (50), Scaup (p.), Goldeneye (immatures), Jays

3rd *no diary entry*

4th Pochards (450), Lapwings, Barn Owls, Short-eared Owls, Long-eared Owls

5th Lapwings, Redwings, Fieldfares

6th Merlins (2), Goldcrests, Wrens

7th Snipe (p.), Jack Snipe (p.), Teal (p.)

8th Pochards (400), Goldeneye (4 immatures), Tufted Ducks (50), Scaup (p.), Great Grey Shrike, Hen-harrier, Merlin

9th Lapwings, Widgeon (4), Pintails (2 f.), Pochards (200), Goldeneye (m. and 7 immatures), Coots

10th *no diary entry*

11th Great Northern Diver (immature), Woodcock, Water Rails, Moorhens

12th Pochards (300), Tufted Ducks, Scaup (p.), Great Crested Grebes (2), Snipe (p.), Merlins (2)

13th Lesser Spotted Woodpecker, Green Woodpeckers (2), Long-tailed Tits, Marsh Tits, Great Tits, Blue Tits

14th Pochards (300), Bewick's Swans (2)

Short-eared owl

15th Lapwings (flocks), Pochards, Mallard (p.), Goldeneye (adult with 7 immatures)

16th Siskins, Lesser Redpolls, Goldfinches, Bullfinches, Rough-legged Buzzard, Hooded Crow, Short-eared Owl

17th Lesser Woodpecker, Goldfinches, Siskins, Lesser Redpolls

18th Goldeneye (adult with 4 immatures), Pochards (350 +), Tufted Ducks (10), Scaup, Teal (20)

19th Woodcock, Barn Owls (2), Jays (6), Long-tailed Tits, Great Tits, Jack Snipe (2), Snipe (p.), Herons, Pochards (200), Coots (1,700)

20th Hen-harrier (f.), Pochards (600), Goldeneye (2 adults with 12 immatures), Tufted Ducks, Black-necked Grebe, Lapwings

21st Pochards, Scaup (p.), Tufted Ducks, Goldeneye (immatures), Great Crested Grebes (2), Dabchick, Bearded Tits

22nd Lapwings (flocks), Pochards (500), Black-necked Grebe, Snipe (p.), Jack Snipe (p.)

23rd Pochards (400), Tufted Ducks (50), Goldeneye (adult with 4 immatures), Geese (flock)

24th–25th *no diary entry*

26th Great Grey Shrike, Blue Tit, Lesser Spotted Woodpeckers (2)

27th Goosanders (2 f.), Tufted Ducks (40), Pochards (200), Lapwings (1000s)

28th Water Rails (5), Moorhens (3), Wood-pigeons (flocks), Teal (8)

29th Mallard (p.), Pochards, Coots, Mistle Thrushes, Song Thrushes

30th Snipe (p.), Hen-harrier (m.), Goldeneye (adult with 13 immatures), Fieldfares

31st *no diary entry*

Some rare birds recorded at Hickling while Jim Vincent was keeper

Yellow-browed Warbler, from Asia (4 May 1928)

Paget's Pochard, from eastern Europe (2 November 1928)

American Widgeon (adult male), from North America (15 September 1931)

Gull-billed Tern, from west coast of Denmark (30 June 1932)

African Serin, from West Africa (24 May 1933)

Spotted Eagle (immature), from eastern Europe (8 March 1934)

Black-tailed Godwit (nest first recorded) (5 June 1934)

Alpine Swift, from Switzerland (4 September 1934)

Rustic Bunting from East Finland (28 April 1935)

Sabine's Gull (immature), from eastern Europe (19 September 1935)

White-winged Black Tern, from Poland (22nd June 1937)

Mutant Wagtail, from eastern Europe (30 June 1941)

Index

Heron